You Want Me to Lead Devotions?!

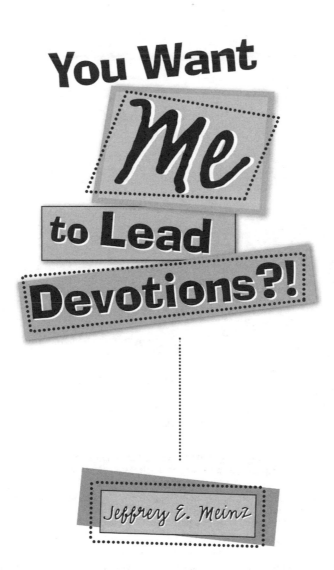

Jeffrey E. Meinz

CONCORDIA PUBLISHING HOUSE • SAINT LOUIS

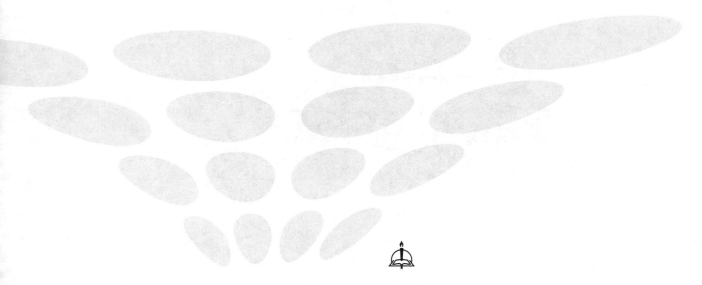

Written by Jeffrey E. Meinz
Edited by Mark S. Sengele

This publication may be available in braille, in large print, or on cassette tape for the visually impaired.
Please allow 8 to 12 weeks for delivery. Write to Lutheran Blind Mission, 7550 Watson Rd., St. Louis, MO 63119-4409;
call toll-free 1-888-215-2455; or visit the Web site: www.blindmission.org.

Manufactured in the United States of America

Your comments and suggestions concerning the material are appreciated. Please write to the Editor of Youth Materials,
Concordia Publishing House, 3558 S. Jefferson Ave., St. Louis, MO 63118-3968.

1 2 3 4 5 6 7 8 9 10   16 15 14 13 12 11 10 09 08 07

Table of Contents

Foreword

As a member of the 2007 LCMS Youth/Adult Gathering planning team, I was asked to lead devotions for a meeting of Gathering planners held in August 2006. The following is that devotion:

When I was asked if I would be willing to lead a devotion at our next meeting, the first thought that came to my mind was, "Why me? Why am I being asked to lead a devotion?" Was I being "chosen" to do this, or was my name simply drawn at random, or was this an example of the "Chosen" theme that I had heard so much about over the last year? Either way, all I could think was, "Why me?"

Perhaps it might help if I explained some things. You see, I have never given a devotion before. I'm not even sure what a devotion truly is, or should be. As many of you may know, I am not a DCE; I'm clearly not a pastor; and I'm not even a paid church worker. I am a layperson, an engineer by trade. I didn't grow up in the Lutheran Church. My parents were Catholic, and we rarely attended church.

I came to the Church through my son, so to speak. When I remarried about eleven years ago, I was looking for a school for my son, and my husband suggested that I check into the Lutheran schools. He had attended a Lutheran school through the sixth grade and recalled what a good education system they had. I enrolled Ryan in the fourth grade at Zion Lutheran School in Belleville, Illinois. I was amazed to see how quickly he took to the teachers, the students, and the religion classes. Our family joined the church a year later and I began my "second career" as a full-time volunteer.

By now, I'm sure some of you are thinking, "What's the big deal? It's only a devotion." Although part of me understood this, I also knew that there are so many others much more qualified to lead a great devotion. But after much prayer and reflection, I now understand that when I ask "Why me, Lord? Why are You calling on me?," I hear God's response when He says, "It's not about you, Sherrill." You see, through my faith journey, God has been kind enough to show me through His Word that I am not alone; He often calls the unlikely or even the unwilling, as He did with Moses, Jonah, Mary, and Paul. And so, the true question should be, "Why *not* me?"

Over this next year, as we continue in our planning, whenever doubt or fear or problems enter our path, we can always draw upon Paul's words to the Philippians when he wrote, "I can do all things through Him who strengthens me" (4:13). Thanks be to God!

Sherrill Smith

Be imitators of GOD, therefore, as dearly loved ch
fe of LOVE, just as Christ loved us and GAVE hir
a fragrant offering and sacrifice to God. (Ephes
ow the plans I have for you,"
o prosper

Introduction

I believe that everyone has the ability to lead group devotions. Devotions are those five-minute meditations conducted just prior to a meeting or event. Devotions set the framework by which we agree to meet: God is present in this place, and we will be Christlike to one another.

When setting out to write this book, I didn't want to write a traditional devotional booklet. You know the kind: You're attending a 7 p.m. meeting for which you've been assigned to lead devotions. At 6:59, you grab the first devotional book on the shelf you see and read the first devotion you open to. I call those "'just add water' devotions." They are as instant as some potatoes.

I wanted this devotional book to be different. I wanted the readers to gain a deeper understanding of who Jesus is. I wanted the devotion leader to plan efficiently and effectively, without spending hours planning for one simple, five-minute devotion.

The devotions in this book are broken up into smaller sections: Scripture Springboard, Activity, Commentary, Personal Story, Concordance, Meditation, and Prayer Springboard. Allow me to explain each section in more detail:

Scripture Springboard

These are the verses from God's Word, the Bible, that will catapult us into a higher place. Just like a diver uses a springboard to launch herself into a complicated dive, God's Word propels us into a greater understanding of Him and His love for us.

Activity

In recent years, we've learned that people learn most effectively by doing. The simple, inexpensive activities in this book enable the listener to gain a different perspective and deeper understanding of what the selected Scripture passage is communicating.

Commentary

These are the thoughts God brought to my mind while I was writing each devotion in this book. Most people think that these must be the "meat and potatoes" of this book. Nothing could be further from the truth. These sections, although the longest, pale in comparison to God's divine Word. The commentaries simply help bring context and insight into the inspired Word of God.

Personal Story

This section makes each devotion different, dynamic, and unique. This is the place where the leader gives a personal touch to the devotion.

I do want to caution you as the leader to take care not to make this devotion suddenly about you. Choose stories that give glory to God and to Him alone. If the most commonly used word in this section is *I*, then you probably want to choose a different story or devotion. Find one that magnifies what Christ did on the cross and in your life. I once heard that "A naked preacher can be very distracting." The point is this: If you expose yourself too much in your stories, the listeners tend to remember only the details of *your* story, and not the pure message from Jesus Christ through His Word.

It is appropriate for you to pray before you lead devotions. I encourage you to ask God to reveal to you whether this devotion is about you or Him. If it's about you, start over.

Concordance

This section is for those who need help finding other verses in Scripture that apply to the devotion being read. The truth is, in today's society, even Christians are far too unfamiliar with God's Word. This fact became more and more evident when I began speaking more in public. At these speaking engagements, I would say, "Turn your Bibles to Genesis." Then I would watch as many in the group opened their Bibles in Revelation and start shuffling through the entire book, all the way to Genesis. It is because of such unfamiliarity with God's Word that I included this simple section.

A concordance is typically in the back of your Bible, or in a separate book. It helps you find a specific verse in Scripture by using key words.

In addition, each Concordance section provides at least one preselected verse that may be used for the Meditation portion of the devotion.

Meditation

Meditation is too often misunderstood in our society. Many associate meditation with sitting in a yoga position while humming some New Age tune and emptying the mind of all thought. Nothing could be further from the truth when it comes to meditating on God's Holy Word.

Meditating on Scripture involves reading the Word; spending time in silence, thinking about the words that have been read; and spending time in prayer. Rather than emptying the mind, the goal of meditating on the Scriptures is to *fill* the mind with the very Word of God.

I am a firm believer in meditating on God's Word. God speaks to you through His Word. Joshua 1:8 says, "This Book of the Law shall not depart from your mouth, but you shall meditate on it day and night, so that you may be careful to do according to all that is written in it. For then you will make your way prosperous, and then you will have good success." To those who study His Word, God promises spiritual blessings. The Spirit of God works through that Word to strengthen our faith and prepare us to face the challenges of living in the world today.

Prayer Springboard

Here is one more opportunity to make the devotion personal. The Prayer Springboard simply begins the prayer for you. You or your entire group can finish it, according to the Spirit's leading. You can gather prayer requests from the group and insert those petitions here. Bottom line: This is your chance to speak to the Creator of the universe from the depths of your heart. Prayer . . . what a privilege and a blessing!

That's it! My prayer for you as the leader is that the group would see God through you and hear His voice. My prayer for you as the listener is that you would receive His Word and apply it to your life by the Spirit's strength.

1

Straightening Out

Scripture Springboard

A voice of one calling: "In the desert prepare the way for the LORD; make straight in the wilderness a highway for our God. Every valley shall be raised up, every mountain and hill made low; the rough ground shall become level, the rugged places a plain. And the glory of the LORD will be revealed, and all mankind together will see it. For the mouth of the LORD has spoken." A voice says, "Cry out." And I said, "What shall I cry?" "All men are like grass, and all their glory is like the flowers of the field" (Isaiah 40:3–6 NIV).

Activity

Give each person a standard metal paper clip. Instruct everyone to unbend their paper clips as straight as possible. You could even declare a winner for the straightest paper clip.

Personal Story

Many of us are familiar with motion sickness. Whether traveling by plane, boat, train, or automobile, we have experienced the discomfort of a queasy stomach. Share a story about a time when you had motion sickness. What happened? When did you feel better? Did you try any remedies from "old wives' tales" to ease your discomfort?

Commentary

Sometimes the only true remedy for motion sickness is solid ground or a straight stretch of smooth highway. Today's Scripture reading encourages us to make straight paths for a different purpose than settling our stomachs. In ancient days, workers were sent ahead of important people to prepare the roads for their arrival. Removing large rocks and filling deep potholes ensured a smooth ride for the honored guest. Jesus is the most honored guest in the life of a Christian. But how prepared are we for His second coming? Is the road littered with sin and sadness? Is it time to "adopt the highway" of our heart and ask God to do a spring cleaning? Psalm 51:10 says, "Create in me a pure heart, O God, and renew a steadfast spirit within me" (NIV). Ask God to reveal to you the slimy pits and places of pride where you dwell. He will lift you up and set your feet upon His rock (Psalm 40:2 NIV).

In His Word, God promises not only to set us upon the right path, but also to forgive our sinfulness and renew us through His Holy Spirit. As we gather for worship, we confess our sins and hear the blessed words of absolution spoken by our pastor. In the Lord's Supper we are forgiven and re-energized to live for, and serve, Christ.

Concordance

Find one more verse that applies to this devotion. Possible key words include *Path, Road, Straight,* and *Prepare.* Or read:

> *"See, I will send My messenger, who will prepare the way before Me. Then suddenly the Lord you are seeking will come to His temple; the messenger of the covenant, whom you desire, will come," says the Lord Almighty (Malachi 3:1 NIV).*

Meditate

Ask participants to listen closely to the final verse and meditate on its meaning. After a couple of moments, close with prayer.

Prayer Springboard

Lord, we admit that we have not fully prepared for Your second arrival. We've been more concerned with our daily lives than the eternity You provide. Forgive us through the death and resurrection of Your Son, Jesus Christ. Renew us by the power of Your Holy Spirit in the Word and Sacraments. . . .

2

That's Frightening!

Scripture Springboard

For you did not receive the spirit of slavery to fall back into fear, but you have received the Spirit of adoption as sons, by whom we cry, "Abba! Father!" The Spirit Himself bears witness with our spirit that we are children of God (Romans 8:15–16).

Activity

Using lightweight rope or string, hang a "clothesline" across the room near where you are having your devotion. Give each person a blank sheet of paper, a pen or pencil, and a clothespin. Allow everyone one minute to draw something that makes them afraid. "You only get one minute, so no masterpieces!" Divide everyone into pairs. Have participants take thirty seconds each to explain to their partner why their drawing leads to fear. Hang the drawings on the clothesline.

Commentary

Think about the last time you were really afraid. Maybe your knees knocked together. Your heart probably raced at twice its normal pace. Your teeth could have chattered or your liver might have quivered.

Personal Story

Tell a brief story about a time that you were really afraid. What happened? How did it get resolved? Did you really need to be afraid after all?

Commentary

When we were young, fear was probably a familiar emotion. Imagine a young child who is afraid of the dark. Often a simple night-light, blanket, or teddy bear will provide the necessary comfort. But for the truly terrified, a comforting mother, father, or other family member can be the only solution.

Today's Scripture encourages us to go to God with our fears. He is our truest Father. Through our Savior Jesus Christ, we were adopted into the family of God at our Baptism. What a comfort to know that when we cry out for any reason, it is God who hears us. Romans 8:31b boldly proclaims, "If God is for us, who can be against us?" (NIV). We read similar promises again and again in God's Word. Take a look at the Book of Psalms, where David and others repeatedly write about the comforting promises of our God.

Most important, Jesus completely defeated sin and Satan by His sacrificial death and glorious resurrection. By faith we are cradled in God's strong, comforting arms. There we can rest securely for all eternity.

Concordance

Find one more verse that applies to this devotion. Possible key words include *Rest*, *Peace*, *Fear*, and *Comfort*. Or read:

Sing for joy, O heavens, and exult, O earth; break forth, O mountains, into singing! for the LORD *has comforted His people and will have compassion on His afflicted (Isaiah 49:13).*

Meditate

Ask participants to listen closely to this final verse and meditate on its meaning. After a couple of moments, close with prayer.

Prayer Springboard

Father God, thank You for adopting us into Your eternal and heavenly family through Your Holy Word and Baptism. It is good to be chosen. It is an honor to be called Your sons and daughters. Because of Jesus Christ, we are no longer slaves to fear. Make us Your servants, Father. . . .

3

Wonderful Work

Scripture Springboard

For You formed my inward parts;
You knitted me together in my
mother's womb. I praise You, for I
am fearfully and wonderfully
made. Wonderful are Your works;
my soul knows it very well (Psalm
139:13–14).

Activity

Have each person take a small lump of modeling clay and mold it into an image (no golden calves, please!). Placing all of the sculptures on a table, have the group guess, one at a time, what each creation is.

_____

_____

_____

_____

_____

_____

_____

_____

_____

Commentary

Every item at an auction was made by someone. Sometimes a single painting sells for thousands or even millions of dollars. By contrast, a box full of dusty trinkets and gadgets might net only a quarter at a Midwestern farm auction. The value of an item often depends on who created it.

Personal Story

Share a story about something that was valuable to you because you knew that someone special had made it. What was it? Where is it now? What do you plan to do with it?

_____

_____

_____

_____

_____

_____

_____

Commentary

Our Scripture reading tells us we are God's artwork, the work of His own hands. Even though God created the entire world—the majestic mountains and the splendid seas—you are His masterpiece, the jewel of His creation. Unfortunately, too often, the creation criticizes the Creator. We do this when we hate ourselves or use our words to criticize others—His works of art hanging in His gallery.

Everyone knows the pain of belittling words. We've all lobbed "verbal bombs" at unsuspecting bystanders and even those we call friends. When we use our words to demean others, we not only hurt them but we cut at the heart of God, the Master Creator. We are not a mass of cells that happened to bond together, forming an earthly being. We were fearfully and wonderfully made in the very image of God (Genesis 1:26). What a thought! When you look in the mirror, you can almost see the fingerprints of God. We are so special to our heavenly Father that He willingly sacrificed His own Son on the cross of Calvary to keep us with Himself for all eternity.

Concordance

Find one more verse that applies to this devotion. Possible key words include *Create*, *Mold*, *Shape*, *Potter*, and *Clay*. Or read:

> *For we are His workmanship,*
> *created in Christ Jesus for good*
> *works, which God prepared*
> *beforehand, that we should walk*
> *in them (Ephesians 2:10).*

Meditate

Ask the participants to listen to the verse you selected and meditate on its meaning. After a couple of moments, close with prayer.

Prayer Springboard

Lord, thank You for creating us in Your image. Forgive us for the times when we don't appreciate ourselves or others. Thank You for the gift of eternal life You give us through the death and resurrection of Jesus, our Savior. Help us to see Your face when we look at other people. . . .

Date used

_____

Used for

_____

4

Temptation All Around

Scripture Springboard

Since we have a great High Priest, Jesus the Son of God, who has gone into heaven, let us hold on to the faith we have. For our High Priest is able to understand our weaknesses. When He lived on earth, He was tempted in every way that we are, but He did not sin. Let us, then, feel very sure that we can come before God's throne where there is grace. There we can receive mercy and grace to help us when we need it (Hebrews 4:14–16).

Activity

Before participants arrive, place a bowl of M&M's on the table. Save the bag; you'll need it later. Count the M&M's so you know how many pieces are in the bowl. Write the number down so you don't forget. On a plain sheet of paper, make a sign that reads, "Do not eat ONE M&M." After reading the Scripture Springboard, ask each student to guess the number of M&M's in the bowl. Whoever guesses closest is the winner. Take the bowl of M&M's and pour them back into the bag.

_____

_____

_____

_____

_____

_____

_____

Commentary

We know from Scripture that David was "a man after His [God's] own heart" (1 Samuel 13:14). We immediately recognize David as the young boy who bravely defeated Goliath. God even made David to be king over Israel. And yet, despite David's godly character, he still gave in to temptation.

Personal Story

Tell of a time when you were tempted. Avoid an intense, bare-all story. A simple account of when you were on a diet and the potato chips in the cupboard kept calling your name will do.

_____

_____

_____

_____

_____

_____

_____

_____

Commentary

When David was king, he used his power to murder Uriah and take his wife so that she could be his own. David gave in to his temptation, and he paid a precious price: the life of his son. In contrast, Jesus was tempted in every way, just as we are. The difference between David, us, and Jesus is that Jesus resisted temptation in every instance. How do we know that to be true? Because our Scripture verses tell us that He was without sin. Remember when Jesus was in the desert at the beginning of His ministry? He was tempted continually by the devil. Jesus battled temptation with Scripture each time (Matthew 4:1–11). I've always wondered why we're always told to memorize verses from the Bible. One of the reasons must be so that we can battle temptation.

By the way, was anyone tempted to eat an M&M earlier? So was I. Probably we all were. Jesus understands that feeling because while being true God, he was also true Man. How comforting it is to know that Jesus empathizes with our humanness. It is even more comforting to know that Jesus' death and resurrection redeem us from all of our sins.

Concordance

Find one more verse that applies to this devotion. Possible key words include _Tempted, Holy, Pure,_ and _Resist._ Or read:

Blessed is the man who remains steadfast under trial, for when he has stood the test he will receive the crown of life, which God has promised to those who love Him. Let no one say when he is tempt-ed, "I am being tempted by God," for God cannot be tempted with evil, and He Himself tempts no one. But each person is tempted when he is lured and enticed by his own desire (James 1:12–14).

_____

_____

_____

_____

_____

_____

_____

Meditate

Listen closely to this final verse and meditate on its meaning. After a couple of moments, close with prayer.

Prayer Springboard

Jesus, it is nearly impossible to go through a single day on this earth without being tempted. You know what that is like. Send Your Spirit through Your Word and Sacraments to give us the strength to resist temptation and cling to You and Your Word during those times. . . .

_____

_____

_____

_____

_____

_____

_____

_____

5

Big Blessings

Scripture Springboard

You are the sons of the prophets and of the covenant that God made with your fathers, saying to Abraham, "And in your offspring shall all the families of the earth be blessed" (Acts 3:25).

Activity

Tape a large piece of poster board or paper onto the wall. Place five markers in the center of the table. Give the group exactly one minute to write down blessings in their lives. After writing each item, they must put the marker back on the table and return to their seats. If a marker is available, someone may get up again. There may be only five people at the poster board at one time. The goal is to get as many blessings as possible written on the poster board in one minute.

_____

_____

_____

_____

_____

_____

_____

_____

Commentary

It doesn't take long to create a lengthy list of blessings given to us by God. If we are honest, we realize that He has given us many more blessings than we'd ever deserve.

Personal Story

Share with the group one blessing that God has given to you. Why is that blessing so important to you? What would life be like without it?

_____

_____

_____

_____

_____

_____

_____

Commentary

Take some time to consider all of the things with which God has blessed you, and reflect on different ways in which you could be a blessing to others through God's gifts to you. Has God given you the gift to play an instrument? Play for God's glory and for the enjoyment of others. Has God blessed you with an abundance of clothes? Share with those around you who are in need. Dear friends, we have been richly blessed. Now we can be the hands of God as a blessing to others.

Why does God so richly bless us? Because we are His children and He loves us deeply. He loves to provide richly when we are in need. Obviously, our greatest need was the need to be freed from the bondage of our sin. God blessed us beyond measure by sending His one and only Son, Jesus, to pay the price of punishment that we deserved. This message of salvation is the greatest blessing we can share with anyone.

Concordance

Find one or more verses that apply to this devotion. Possible key words include *Blessed*, *Help*, and *Need*. Or read:

> *"Blessed is the man who trusts in the LORD, whose trust is the LORD. He is like a tree planted by water, that sends out its roots by the stream, and does not fear when heat comes, for its leaves remain green, and is not anxious in the year of drought, for it does not cease to bear fruit" (Jeremiah 17:7–8).*

Meditate

Ask participants to meditate on one of the verses you found and its meaning. After a couple of moments, close with prayer.

Prayer Springboard

Dear God, the Great Provider, thank You for all of the blessings You have given to us. We thank You most for the blessings of forgiveness and salvation earned by Jesus on the cross and granted to us through faith at our Baptism. According to Your perfect will, reveal to us where we can help, serve, and be a blessing to those around us. . . .

Date used

_____

Used for

6

Fighting the Battle

Scripture Springboard

This day the LORD will deliver you into my hand . . . that all the earth may know that there is a God in Israel, and that all this assembly may know that the LORD saves not with sword and spear. For the battle is the LORD's, and He will give you into our hand (1 Samuel 17:46–47).

Activity

Give every person two blank note cards and a marker. Ask two volunteers to participate in a good, old-fashioned pillow fight. Make sure that you have adequate room for this activity and there is nothing breakable nearby. Have each person write the names of the "fighters" on their cards. The pillow fight will last for three thirty-second rounds. After each round, have everyone vote by holding up the card with the name of the fighter who they thought won that round.

_____

_____

_____

_____

Commentary

You may have heard a quote similar to this one: "Be kind to everyone you meet, because we're all fighting a tough battle." Each one of us probably is wrestling right now with something—or someone—in our life.

Personal Story

Share with the group a "battle" you fought or are fighting.

_____

_____

_____

_____

_____

Commentary

There is one battle we do not need to fight: the battle for our salvation. Jesus won that battle nearly two thousand years ago when He came out of the grave. We know that immediately after His death on the cross, Jesus descended into hell. Why? For a victory lap! He wanted to look Satan squarely in the eyes and proclaim, "You lost. I won!"

Despite the fact that our salvation through faith in Jesus is solid and secure, life still seems tough sometimes. Friends and family members still pass away. You didn't make the track team . . . You didn't get the job you wanted . . . The list goes on and on. The world has thousands of "bumper-sticker messages" they want you to hear. "When the going gets tough, the tough get going."

Scripture reminds us that our battles, big and small, belong to the Lord. We turn them over to Him and ask Him to create the master battle plan. Since we are His soldiers, dressed in the full armor of God, He loves to share the plan with us: "Be in My Word, seek My kingdom, pray, and love your Lord. The battle still may not be easy, but the Commander-in-Chief will remain by your side every step of the way. He has already won the battle for us on the cross. We have the victory over our worst enemies—sin, death, and the devil."

Concordance

Find one more verse that applies to this devotion. Possible key words include *Battle*, *Fight*, *Victory*, and *Salvation*. Or read:

Behold! I tell you a mystery. We shall not all sleep, but we shall all be changed, in a moment, in the twinkling of an eye, at the last trumpet. For the trumpet will sound, and the dead will be raised imperishable, and we shall be changed. For this perishable body must put on the imperishable, and this mortal body must put on immortality. When the perishable puts on the imperishable, and the mortal puts on

immortality, then shall come to pass the saying that is written: "Death is swallowed up in victory. O death, where is your victory? O death, where is your sting?" The sting of death is sin, and the power of sin is the law. But thanks be to God, who gives us the victory through our Lord Jesus Christ (1 Corinthians 15:51–57).

Meditate

Listen closely to the selected verse and meditate on its meaning. After a couple of moments, close with prayer.

Prayer Springboard

Have each person find a partner and share the battles they are currently fighting. Give them two minutes for this—one minute each. Encourage each person to really listen to his partner. End this devotion by allowing partners to pray for each other's battles, reminding them that the ultimate battle already has been won in Christ's defeat of Satan and his evil ones.

7

Anger Issues

Scripture Springboard

Know this, my beloved brothers:
let every person be quick to hear,
slow to speak, slow to anger; for
the anger of man does not pro-
duce the righteousness that God
requires (James 1:19–20).

Activity

Bring enough cans of soda so everyone in your group can have one can. With the can in hand, have the students shout out as many descriptive words as they can about the can or the soda. After one minute, allow the students to vigorously shake their cans of soda. Are there any changes to the can or its contents? Does anyone want to open their can? Why not? What would happen? (NOTE: Some students may know that you *can* safely open the just-shaken can of soda if you first snap the side of the can with your fingers.)

_____

_____

_____

_____

_____

Commentary

Anger is a messy business. Frustrations, building up pressure over time, can only do one thing—explode! The mess resulting from our hotheadedness often leads to embarrassment and, one would hope, a repentant heart.

Personal Story

Share a time when you became angry about something. What made you so angry? Did you explode? How did you feel afterward? What mess was left behind to clean up after your episode of anger? Ultimately, was there forgiveness?

_____

_____

_____

_____

_____

Commentary

Sometimes you don't get the things you desire. Or you've been lied to one too many times. You've been called a name repeatedly. They just keep yelling and yelling. You hit your thumb with a hammer. A passing car splashes muddy rainwater on your outfit. These aren't the only things that lead to anger. Emotions often result in a familiar rage: anxiety, stress, chaos. Anger is a bomb that must be defused.

Elijah was no stranger to anger. Look at 1 Kings 19:10, which tells how Elijah yelled at God: "I have been very zealous for the Lord God Almighty. The Israelites have rejected Your covenant, broken down Your altars, and put Your prophets to death with the sword. I am the only one left, and now they are trying to kill me too" (NIV). How did God respond? He answered with a gentle, caressing whisper of wind. He came to Elijah in his time of need.

When anger threatens to steal our joy, God invites us to come near to Him (James 4:8). God promises to rescue us and those around us from anger. Through His Word and Sacraments, God sends us His Holy Spirit to bring a peace only He can provide.

Concordance

Find one or more verses that apply to this devotion. Possible key words include *Anger*, *Patience*, and *Compassion*. Or read:

"In overflowing anger for a moment I hid My face from you, but with everlasting love I will have compassion on you," says the Lord, your Redeemer. "This is like the days of Noah to Me: as I swore that the waters of Noah should no more go over the earth, so I have sworn that I will not be angry with you, and will not rebuke you. For the mountains may depart and the hills be removed, but My steadfast love shall not depart from you, and My covenant of peace shall not be removed," says the Lord, who has compassion on you (Isaiah 54:8–10).

_____

_____

_____

_____

_____

Meditate

Ask participants to meditate on the meaning of the verses you select. After a couple of moments, close with prayer.

Prayer Springboard

Lord, we admit that we too often choose anger instead of peace and patience. Forgive us, for Jesus' sake, for those times. Through Your Word and Sacraments, give us Your peace through the Holy Spirit, and help us to . . . .

_____

_____

_____

_____

_____

21

8

Pump You Up!

Scripture Springboard

For the foolishness of God is wiser than men, and the weakness of God is stronger than men (1 Corinthians 1:25).

Activity

Ask for two volunteers. Give each an identical heavy item (dumbbell, gallon of water, etc.). Tell them that you are going to find out who is the stronger person of the two. Tell them to begin "curling" the heavy item and continue until one person gives up. Giving the winner a badge, trophy, or ribbon would leave a lasting impression.

Commentary

Our world is filled with things that want to make you stronger: protein shakes, powders, machines, fitness clubs, and, unfortunately, even illegal drugs.

Personal Story

Tell about a time when you tried to become stronger. Perhaps share a story about when you displayed a certain physical strength.

Commentary

Many people spend hour after hour in fitness centers and weight rooms. Some of them aren't there to lose weight, but to gain muscle—a lot of it. Why? Are they preparing for the day when they might need to lift a car off of their mother? Are they getting ready to displace a tree from the ground with one yank? Probably not; in fact, my guess is that some of those people are just trying to be stronger than the next guy or gal.

But there is one person they will never outmuscle—God. Imagine if you could gather the thousand strongest people in the world and challenge God to a tug-of-war. The competition would be over in less than a second. God would reign victorious, just as He always does.

The Old Testament records the story of Jacob wrestling with God (Genesis 32:24–32). Jacob fought with God with all his strength throughout the night, but with a single touch of His hand, God dislocated Jacob's hip.

This same all-powerful God cares deeply about you and me. 2 Corinthians 12:9–10 says, "But He said to me, 'My grace is sufficient for you, for My power is made perfect in weakness.' Therefore I will boast all the more gladly of my weaknesses, so that the power of Christ may rest upon me. For the sake of Christ, then, I am content with weaknesses, insults, hardships, persecutions, and calamities. For when I am weak, then I am strong." It is only when we realize our powerlessness before God that we really begin to understand His grace toward us. On our own we can do nothing, so God does it all for us. Through the suffering, death, and resurrection of Christ, He freely gives us life and salvation for all eternity.

Concordance

Find one additional Bible verse that applies to this devotion. Possible key words include *Strength*, *Power*, and *Weakness*. Or read:

> *Now to Him who is able to do immeasurably more than all we ask or imagine, according to His power that is at work within us, to Him be glory in the church and in Christ Jesus throughout all generations, for ever and ever! Amen (Ephesians 3:20–21 NIV).*

_____

_____

_____

_____

_____

Meditate

Listen closely to the final verse and meditate on its meaning. After a couple of moments, close with prayer.

> *The LORD is my strength and my song, and He has become my salvation; this is my God, and I will praise Him, my father's God, and I will exalt Him (Exodus 15:2).*

Prayer Springboard

Dear almighty God, we praise You this day because of Your strength and Your power. We thank You that through the power of Christ, You grant us eternal life. Please protect us this day according to Your perfect will and Your mighty power. . . .

_____

_____

_____

_____

_____

9

Future Focus

Scripture Springboard

"For I know the plans I have for you," declares the LORD, "plans to prosper you and not to harm you, plans to give you hope and a future. Then you will call upon Me and come and pray to Me, and I will listen to you" (Jeremiah 29:11 NIV).

Activity

Ask this question: "What does your life look like in five years?" Go around the room and give each person a moment to contemplate his five-year vision. Let each participant briefly share his vision of his future.

_____

_____

_____

_____

_____

_____

_____

_____

Commentary

Of course, no one really knows what his future holds. But for Christians, it is clear who holds our future. With God as our guide, our future is secure.

Personal Story

Tell about a time when you had "perfect" plans that didn't turn out the way you expected. What was supposed to happen? What really happened? Did it work out better than you had planned?

_____

_____

_____

_____

_____

_____

_____

Commentary

Our Scripture reading today reminds us that God wants the very best for you and me, His children. No parent is a stranger to this feeling. Every mother and father wants the very best for their children. It is the same way with our Father, God. He does not desire hurt for us; rather, He plans for our prosperity. God wants nothing more than for us to succeed.

But our sin forms a barrier between us and the riches God desires us to have through Him. With every step we try to take, bogged down in the muck and mire of sin, we lose hope for the future. We can only focus on our failure. But God made a way through His perfect Son, Jesus Christ. Because of Jesus, we have a future that never ends. Heaven is our eternal home because God willingly gave His only Son as our Savior. The "hope and future" God prepares is an indescribable one—beyond our earthly imagination. Spending eternity with our Savior, Jesus, is the greatest hope of all.

Concordance

Find a few verses that apply to this devotion. Possible key words include *Future*, *Heaven*, *Hope*, and *Plans*. Or read:

> *Our soul waits for the LORD; He is our help and our shield. For our heart is glad in Him, because we trust in His holy name. Let Your steadfast love, O LORD, be upon us, even as we hope in You (Psalm 33:20–22).*

Meditate

Have participants meditate on the meaning of one or more verses. After a couple of moments, close with prayer.

Prayer Springboard

Lord, You long to bring us home to Yourself. Through the holy life, innocent death, and glorious resurrection of Your own Son, Jesus, You make this possible. Help us to know the plans You have laid out for us. . . .

10

Lost and Found

Scripture Springboard

"Ask and it will be given to you; seek and you will find; knock and the door will be opened to you. For everyone who asks receives; he who seeks finds; and to him who knocks, the door will be opened" (Matthew 7:7–8 NIV).

Activity

Before your event, set an alarm clock to go off one or two minutes after the start of your devotion. Hide the alarm clock in the room or building. After reading the Scripture Springboard, explain to the group that an alarm is about to go off. The first person to find the clock wins.

Commentary

Everyone knows the frustration of losing something. Sometimes you find yourself scurrying around the house, looking for your keys, or digging through your desk, looking for an important document.

Personal Story

Tell about a time when you lost something important. What was it? Have you found it yet? How did you feel when you realized you had lost it?

Commentary

Sometimes we seek something because of a void or emptiness in our lives. It can be as simple as seeking a sandwich to fill your empty stomach, or as intense as seeking a birth parent decades after adoption. In today's Scripture reading, Jesus realizes that the earthly people He created have real needs. Jesus is ready, willing, and incredibly able to give you the "good gifts" (Matthew 7:11) that you really need according to His perfect will and precise timing. Yet even these gifts are temporary.

We also know the frustration of losing something. Perhaps you have had the joy of finding such a lost item. But that joy cannot begin to compare with the joy recorded in the Gospel of Luke. Moved by the Holy Spirit, Luke records three parables concerning lost items (Luke 15). As each parable concludes, Luke records a picture of the celebration in heaven over one repentant sinner (Luke 15:7, 10). We, too, were lost in our sin. Through His Word and the Sacrament of Holy Baptism, God seeks and saves us from the power of the devil, making us His for all eternity—and the angels in heaven rejoice!

Concordance

Find one more verse that applies to this devotion. Possible key words include *Seek*, *Look*, and *Find*. Or read:

> *If then you have been raised with Christ, seek the things that are above, where Christ is, seated at the right hand of God. Set your minds on things that are above, not on things that are on earth. For you have died, and your life is hidden with Christ in God. When Christ who is your life appears, then you also will appear with Him in glory (Colossians 3:1–4).*

Meditate

Have participants listen closely to the final verse and meditate on its meaning. After a couple of moments, close with prayer.

Prayer Springboard

Jesus, You know even better than we do the things that we really need. Through Your suffering, death, and resurrection You gave us the gift of salvation. Help us to separate our needs from our wants. By Your Spirit, help us to ask with pure desires. May Your will be done in our lives. . . .

11

Lights Out!

Scripture Springboard

You are the light of the world. A city set on a hill cannot be hidden. Nor do people light a lamp and put it under a basket, but on a stand, and it gives light to all in the house. In the same way, let your light shine before others, so that they may see your good works and give glory to your Father who is in heaven (Matthew 5:14–16).

Activity

Place a lit votive or tea light candle in front of each participant. Give everyone an inexpensive water gun like those available at most party supply and discount stores. Tell participants that the objective of this game is to use their water guns to extinguish the candles of every other person without leaving their seats. In no way may participants touch, defend, or shield their own candles. When their candle goes out, they are out of the game and may not shoot at other candles. The last person whose candle remains lit is declared the winner. Move that candle to the center of the table.

Commentary

It's evening and the storm pounds your home with incredible force. The power fails and your anxiety peaks as you're crippled by darkness. What's the first thing you must find? A candle or a flashlight (preferably one with brand-new batteries) is your only immediate source of comfort.

Personal Story

Tell about a time when you were in a dark place. What was the first light you saw? How did you feel in the dark? How did you feel when you saw the light?

_____

_____

_____

_____

workmanship, created in Christ
Jesus to do good works, which
God prepared in advance for us to
do (Ephesians 2:8–10 NIV).

Commentary

It's no surprise that we live in a spiritually dark world. Just turn on the evening news and you'll hear about an abandoned baby found in a dumpster or a shooting in a local grocery store. No Christian would argue the fact that this shadowy world needs to see the bright light of Jesus.

That's where we come in. In His wisdom, God placed us in the world to be reflections of His light. What does that mean? It means that we are to stand out from the rest of the crowd. Matthew 5:16 says it clearly: "Let your light shine before others, so that they may see your good works and give glory to your Father who is in heaven." The world will know that we are Christians by our deeds, by our actions.

It deserves to be said that we don't practice good deeds for the sake of salvation. In fact, on our own, we cannot perform even one good deed. Rather, Jesus earned our salvation on the cross once and for all. Through His Holy Spirit, given at our Baptism, God empowers us to perform acts of kindness toward others. These good deeds are our response to God for the wonderful gifts of faith and eternal life. So we can let our lights shine boldly—not for our glory, but for His.

Concordance

Find one more verse that applies to this devotion. Possible key words include *Light*, *Darkness*, *Candle*, and *Deeds*. Or read:

> *For it is by grace you have been*
> *saved, through faith—and this*
> *not from yourselves, it is the gift*
> *of God—not by works, so that no*
> *one can boast. For we are God's*

Meditate

Read aloud your selected verse, encouraging participants to meditate on its meaning. After a couple of moments, close with prayer.

Prayer Springboard

Heavenly Father, thank You for sending Your Son, Jesus Christ, as our Savior from sin. Help us to let our lights shine for Your glory. By Your Spirit, allow us to see the works You have prepared in advance for us to do. . . .

_____

_____

_____

_____

_____

12

Empty on Easter

Scripture Springboard

But the angel said to the women, "Do not be afraid, for I know that you seek Jesus who was crucified. He is not here, for He has risen, as He said. Come, see the place where He lay" (Matthew 28:5–6).

Activity

Gather as many plastic Easter eggs as you can. Before your event, hide them throughout the room where you will gather. Don't worry about putting them in obvious places. In one of the eggs, place a small scrap of paper or a dollar bill. Explain to the group that they need to find as many eggs as possible and return to their seats in one minute. After they have returned to their seats, explain that one egg has something in it. Whoever has that egg is the winner. Ask, "What was it like to find the egg with something in it?" Also ask, "What was it like to open egg after egg and find nothing, only emptiness?"

Commentary

We've all experienced it: an empty cookie jar, an empty wallet, an empty checkbook, an empty relationship. We all desire these things to be full, and we are disappointed when we find them empty.

Personal Story

Share a time when you found something empty that you hoped would be full. What was it? Where had the contents gone? How did you feel when you discovered emptiness?

Commentary

Emptiness often leads to a bare, vacant feeling. That void we experience can be created by an empty promise or by feeling emotionally, even spiritually, empty. It's no surprise that Mary Magdalene and the other Mary felt such alarm. Forget the angel, the earthquake, and the rolled-away rock. The tomb was empty! Remember, this was their first Easter. They didn't know the rest of the story. They must have wondered, "Where is the body of Jesus?" "Who has taken His body?" "Where did they take the fallen body of my Lord?" There seemed to be far too many questions and far too few answers.

The women were no strangers to emptiness. Sure, they knew the familiar sight of an empty flour bowl or oil jar. But try to imagine the emptiness their hearts felt when their Savior had been violently crucified on the cross. So why did the angel tell the women to "fear not"? The angel needed to remind the women, and us, that even though the tomb was empty, Jesus' promises were not. "He has risen, as He said," the angel proclaimed. The women immediately learned that Easter didn't mean emptiness. It meant God's promise fulfilled through Jesus, our Savior.

Concordance

Find more verses that apply to this devotion. Possible key words include *Empty*, *Filled*, *Tomb*, and *Raised*. Or read:

Blessed be the Lord God of Israel,
for He has visited and redeemed
His people and has raised up a
horn of salvation for us in the
house of His servant David, as He
spoke by the mouth of His holy
prophets from of old, that we
should be saved from our enemies
and from the hand of all who
hate us (Luke 1:68–71).

Meditate

Meditate on the meaning of some of the verses you find. After a couple of moments, close with prayer.

Prayer Springboard

Dear Jesus, thank You for Your resurrection from the grave. We praise You that through the empty tomb, You gained eternal life in heaven for us. Through Your Word, reassure us once again of Your love and care for us. . . .

13

The Yoke's on You

Scripture Springboard

Come to Me, all who labor and are heavy laden, and I will give you rest. Take My yoke upon you, and learn from Me, for I am gentle and lowly in heart, and you will find rest for your souls. For My yoke is easy, and My burden is light (Matthew 11:28–30).

Activity

Before your event, find as many heavy books as you can (an old set of encyclopedias would be perfect). Ask for a volunteer, and then load your volunteer down, one book at a time. Before handing him each book, ask, "Are you all right? Can I add another book?" Eventually the stack will become too heavy, and he will drop the books onto the floor. Ask, "What was this experience like for you?"

_____
_____
_____
_____
_____
_____
_____

Commentary

Step after painful step, we trudge through life with the weight of the world on our shoulders. The burden becomes heavier and heavier, and sweat begins to bead on our furrowed brow.

Personal Story

Talk about a time when you carried a heavy burden, either physically, mentally, or emotionally. What was that like? Do you still carry that load today? If not, how was the burden lifted?

_____
_____
_____
_____
_____
_____

Commentary

In the midst of our burdened journey, we beg and we plead for someone to help. We yearn for someone, *anyone*, to please take a pound or two of our lumbering load. How quickly we forget that Jesus offered us His lighter yoke, days, decades, even centuries before we were born. If anyone in the world could empathize with our baggage, it is the Son of God, who walked on this earth as true man. Furthermore, the weight He carried included far more than our earthly burdens. He also carried our sins.

Our Savior and Brother still offers a lighter yoke to us today. In His Word, He bids us to come to Him, and He will give us rest. Through God's free gift of faith, we receive the yoke that Christ gives, and we feel the peace only He can provide.

Concordance

Find one more verse that applies to this devotion. Possible key words include *Yoke*, *Burden*, *Rest*, and *Weary*. Or read:

> *Even youths shall faint and be weary, and young men shall fall exhausted; but they who wait for the LORD shall renew their strength; they shall mount up with wings like eagles; they shall run and not be weary; they shall walk and not faint (Isaiah 40:30–31).*

_____

_____

_____

_____

_____

Meditate

Listen closely to the Scripture passage and meditate on its meaning. After a couple of moments, close with prayer.

Prayer Springboard

Thank You, dear Father, for providing us with a time of rest. Help us to release from our grip the burdens that we choose to bear. . . .

_____

_____

_____

_____

_____

_____

_____

_____

_____

_____

14

Do You Understand?

Scripture Springboard

I pray that out of His glorious riches He may strengthen you with power through His Spirit in your inner being, so that Christ may dwell in your hearts through faith. And I pray that you, being rooted and established in love, may have power, together with all the saints, to grasp how wide and long and high and deep is the love of Christ, and to know this love that surpasses knowledge— that you may be filled to the measure of all the fullness of God (Ephesians 3:16–19 NIV).

Activity

Bring all the ingredients that you'll need to make a batch of chocolate-chip cookies. Explain to the group that precise measurements will be the key to baking the cookies successfully. Mix the cookies using the precise amount of each ingredient called for. When the dough is ready, you could prepare a pan of cookies for the oven (if available) and then enjoy warm chocolate-chip cookies for a snack when your event is over.

Commentary

Imagine a teacher who hands an advanced algebra test to a room full of first-grade students and expects them to get perfect scores. Imagine giving a computer to a person who can't tell the difference between a monitor and a keyboard and expect him to perfect a PowerPoint presentation by noon.

Personal Story

Tell about a time when you tried to understand something and couldn't. What were you trying to grasp? Why couldn't you obtain the knowledge?

Commentary

Many people feel it is impossible to ever understand the love God has for us. They feel comfortable simply knowing the basic "Jesus loves me, this I know." As we mature and grow physically, the Holy Spirit works through God's Word to help us grow in our faith and spiritual understanding. The apostle Paul experienced the changing effects of God's grace in dramatic fashion. Paul says:

I pray that out of His glorious riches He may strengthen you with power through His Spirit in your inner being, so that Christ may dwell in your hearts through faith. And I pray that you, being rooted and established in love, may have power, together with all the saints, to grasp how wide and long and high and deep is the love of Christ, and to know this love that surpasses knowledge— that you may be filled to the measure of all the fullness of God (Ephesians 3:16–19 NIV).

This side of heaven, we will never fully understand the extent of God's love in Christ. We can, however, learn from examples recorded in Scripture. In his First Letter to the Church at Corinth, Paul writes:

When I was a child, I spoke like a child, I thought like a child, I reasoned like a child. When I became a man, I gave up childish ways. For now we see in a mirror dimly, but then face to face. Now I know in part; then I shall know fully, even as I have been fully known (1 Corinthians 13:11–12).

Concordance

Find one or more verses that apply to this devotion. Possible key words include *Filled*, *Fullness*, *Love*, and *Measure*. Or read:

He is the image of the invisible God, the firstborn of all creation.

For by Him all things were created, in heaven and on earth, visible and invisible, whether thrones or dominions or rulers or authorities—all things were created through Him and for Him. And He is before all things, and in Him all things hold together. And He is the head of the body, the church. He is the beginning, the firstborn from the dead, that in everything He might be preeminent. For in Him all the fullness of God was pleased to dwell, and through Him to reconcile to Himself all things, whether on earth or in heaven, making peace by the blood of His cross. And you, who once were alienated and hostile in mind, doing evil deeds, He has now reconciled in His body of flesh by His death, in order to present you holy and blameless and above reproach before Him (Colossians 1:15–22).

Meditate

Ask the participants to listen closely to the selected verse and meditate on its meaning. After a couple of moments, close with prayer.

Prayer Springboard

Loving Father, we thank You for sending Jesus to save us from our sins. We pray that You would send Your powerful Spirit through Your Word to enable us to better understand Your love for us. . . .

15

Busy-ness

Scripture Springboard

But the Lord answered her, "Martha, Martha, you are anxious and troubled about many things, but one thing is necessary. Mary has chosen the good portion, which will not be taken away from her" (Luke 10:41–42).

Activity

Give each person a sheet of lined paper. Allow one minute for each person to prepare a "to do" list—"Fold the laundry," "Wash the dog," "Change the oil in the car," and so forth. Have participants share their lists with their neighbors and look for common threads. Maybe they'll bump into each other at the car wash!

_____

_____

_____

_____

_____

_____

_____

Commentary

Busy, busy, busy. Our world is full of people who are always on the go. Where are we rushing off to? What are we doing? Out lists grow longer and longer, and it seems that they are rarely, if ever, completed.

Personal Story

Tell the group about a distasteful task that continually appears on your "to do" list. What about the task do you dislike? Why do you keep doing it?

_____

_____

_____

_____

_____

_____

_____

Commentary

Martha, the sister of Mary, was no stranger to doing. When Jesus came to visit, she was "distracted with much serving." We imagine her cooking and cleaning. Mary, on the other hand, was sitting at the feet of the Savior, listening. Imagine her eyes as she looked intently at Jesus, the Christ.

It is possible to apply these words of Scripture to our lives at church. In our sinful busy-ness, we can get so wrapped up in the preparations and activities that we lose sight of the true focus, Jesus Christ. We are thankful that God, in Christ, forgives us and encourages us to spend time with Him. Psalm 46:10 encourages us to "Be still, and know that I am God." Instead of "be still," some biblical translators say simply, "cease striving." What a wonderful reminder! On our own we cannot strive toward God; rather, He comes to us in His Word and Sacraments to strengthen us for service to Him.

Concordance

Find one more verse that applies to this devotion. Possible key words include *Praise, Sit,* and *Feet.* Or read:

> *Be still before the* LORD *and wait patiently for Him; fret not yourself over the one who prospers in his way, over the man who carries out evil devices (Psalm 37:7)!*

Meditate

Listen closely to this final verse and meditate on its meaning. After a couple of moments, close with prayer.

Prayer Springboard

Dear God, You have done so much for us, giving us Your only Son, Jesus, as our Savior from sin. By Your Spirit, help us focus our eyes on You, and on Your Word. . . .

37

16

Necessary Departure

Scripture Springboard

Nevertheless, I tell you the truth: it is to your advantage that I go away, for if I do not go away, the Helper will not come to you. But if I go, I will send Him to you (John 16:7).

Activity

Ask one person in your group to go out into the hallway. Have one of the remaining people hide somewhere in the room (in a closet, behind a couch, etc.). After the person is hidden, invite the first person back into the room and have him guess who is missing from the group. Who went away? Who disappeared?

_____

_____

_____

_____

_____

_____

_____

Commentary

Family gatherings are often too short. Fellowship with brother, sister, father, and mother are blessed experiences that can lead to fond memories. Imagine how the disciples must have felt when their friend and brother Jesus announced His imminent departure.

Personal Story

Tell about a time when a dear friend or family member moved away or left for a significant amount of time. Who was it? Where did he go? When was the last time you saw him? How did his departure make you feel?

_____

_____

_____

_____

_____

_____

_____

Commentary

When Jesus spoke the words recorded in John's Gospel, the disciples' minds must have been silently screaming, "Jesus, we thought You would be with us forever!" But when Jesus spoke these words, He knew that He had "places to go and people to see," as the old expression goes. Jesus knew that He was about to begin His journey to the cross, where He would pay the price for your sin and mine. Following His resurrection, the disciples begin to understand the journey Christ was making. One day soon, He would leave them to take His rightful seat at the right hand of the Father. But Jesus did not leave His disciples or us alone. On Pentecost the disciples received the gift of the Holy Spirit. You and I receive that same gift at our Baptism. The Spirit continues to work within us as we read and study God's Word. God never left us, and He never will.

Concordance

Find additional verses that apply to this devotion. Possible key words include *Spirit*, *Counselor*, and *Comforter*. Or read:

> *But the Counselor, the Holy Spirit, whom the Father will send in My name, will teach you all things and will remind you of everything I have said to you (John 14:26 NIV).*

Meditate

Allow time for participants to meditate on the meaning of these words of Scripture. After a couple of moments, close with prayer.

Prayer Springboard

Holy Spirit, Counselor, we thank and praise You for Your presence. Guide and direct us as we study Your Holy Word. . . .

17

Armed, but Dangerous

Scripture Springboard

Finally, be strong in the Lord and in the strength of His might. Put on the whole armor of God, that you may be able to stand against the schemes of the devil. For we do not wrestle against flesh and blood, but against the rulers, against the authorities, against the cosmic powers over this present darkness, against the spiritual forces of evil in the heavenly places . . . praying at all times in the Spirit, with all prayer and supplication. To that end keep alert with all perseverance, making supplication for all the saints (Ephesians 6:10–12, 18).

Activity

Bring enough dolls or action figures so that each pair of participants can use one. Also give each pair aluminum foil, scissors, tape, and cardboard. While reading Ephesians 6:13–17, give each pair a few minutes to dress their figure in the full armor of God. When everyone is done, host a quick "fashion show."

_____

_____

_____

_____

_____

_____

Commentary

A thin sliver of the sun rises over the distant horizon. Christian warriors are dressing for the battle ahead. The body bears more and more weight as each piece of armor is strapped, buckled, and tied into place. The battle is about to begin—against one another.

Personal Story

Tell a brief story about a time when you and a fellow Christian had a disagreement and found forgiveness. What was the issue? How was it resolved?

_____

_____

_____

_____

_____

_____

_____

_____

Commentary

Scripture is clear; the purpose of putting on the armor described in Ephesians is to prepare us for battle against the devil and his evil forces. Yet day in and day out, we suit up in God's armor, and then look for a neighbor, brother, or friend to attack. We scream hateful things at one another and whisper gossip to a world of waiting ears. As humans, we search out conflict like it's a priceless gem in an untapped mine. We long for the "soap operas" in our life, because without them, life would be boring and dull. All the while, the devil snickers in delight as the target shifts from himself and onto fellow believers. It amazes me how much effort we put into wounding one another when the devil is our real enemy. But we cannot take him on alone. We need the weapon listed among the pieces of armor. God's Word calls us to arm ourselves with the sword of the Spirit, which is the very Word of God. Strengthened by the power of the risen Christ, in Word and Sacrament, we are prepared to take on the enemy.

Concordance

Find one more verse that applies to this devotion. Possible key words include *Battle*, *Armor*, *War*, and *Victory*. Or read:

> *When the perishable puts on the imperishable, and the mortal puts on immortality, then shall come to pass the saying that is written: "Death is swallowed up in victory. O death, where is your victory? O death, where is your sting?" The sting of death is sin, and the power of sin is the law. But thanks be to God, who gives us the victory through our Lord Jesus Christ (1 Corinthians 15:54–57).*

Meditate

Listen closely to this final verse and meditate on its meaning. After a couple of moments, close with prayer.

Prayer Springboard

Jesus, forgive us for the times when we forget who the enemy really is. Send us Your Spirit in Word and Sacrament to strengthen us for the battle against the evil one. . . .

Date used

Used for

18

Gushing

Scripture Springboard

And the LORD said to Moses, "Pass on before the people, taking with you some of the elders of Israel, and take in your hand the staff with which you struck the Nile, and go. Behold, I will stand before you there on the rock at Horeb, and you shall strike the rock, and water shall come out of it, and the people will drink." And Moses did so (Exodus 17:5–6).

Activity

Conduct a quick "rock, paper, scissors" tournament. Have everyone stand and find a partner and begin the tournament. When participants lose, they should sit down. The winners should play against each other until there are only two people left; then pause for the championship round.

Commentary

An intense need was filled in the most unlikely of places. The elders stood, stared, and were shocked at the spewing stone. Imagine the faces of the Israelite people. "Quail and manna and now this! Somebody pinch me! I must be dreaming!" Think about all the men, women, children, and livestock that needed to drink. You can almost imagine Moses standing there, counting to five for each person before the next person could drink, just like your grade-school teacher used to do.

Personal Story

Share a story about a time when God filled an extreme need in your life. Remember that God sometimes uses ordinary things and people to achieve amazing results.

Commentary

As the children of Israel stared in amazement at the gushing rock, they didn't realize that this wouldn't be the last rock that would fill a need in their lives. They hardly could have imagined that one day, the Rock of Ages, Jesus, would be struck with a spear, and water would flow once again. "But one of the soldiers pierced His side with a spear, and at once there came out blood and water" (John 19:34). This time it wasn't simply a human thirst caused by lack of water. Rather, we all needed a Savior from the crushing "thirst" of sin. Once again God provided, this time by sending His only Son as our Rock and Redeemer.

God has and will continue to be the Great Provider. God longs to provide for His chosen people, whether they are hungry and thirsty desert wanderers or sinners like you and me. Have a need? Call and wait upon the Lord. Another miracle could be just around the corner.

Concordance

Find a few verses that apply to this devotion. Possible key words include *Rock*, *Provide*, and *Give*. Or read:

What then shall we say? That the Gentiles, who did not pursue righteousness, have obtained it, a righteousness that is by faith; but Israel, who pursued a law of righteousness, has not attained it. Why not? Because they pursued it not by faith but as if it were by works. They stumbled over the "stumbling stone." As it is written: "See, I lay in Zion a stone that causes men to stumble and a rock that makes them fall, and the one who trusts in Him will never be put to shame" (Romans 9:30–33 NIV).

Meditate

Ask participants to listen closely to this final verse and meditate on its meaning. After a couple of moments, close with prayer.

Prayer Springboard

Dear God, the Great Provider, what more could we ask of You? You have blessed us beyond measure, more than we could ever deserve. Thank You for sending the Rock, Jesus Christ, Your only Son, as our Savior. . . .

19

Famished

Scripture Springboard

Then He ordered the crowds to sit down on the grass, and taking the five loaves and the two fish, He looked up to heaven and said a blessing. Then He broke the loaves and gave them to the disciples, and the disciples gave them to the crowds. And they all ate and were satisfied. And they took up twelve baskets full of the broken pieces left over. And those who ate were about five thousand men, besides women and children (Matthew 14:19–21).

Activity

Give each person a clean, white paper plate. Provide several markers. Ask participants to use the markers to draw and label their plates with their perfect meal. Encourage them to include amounts like "heaping pile" or "morsel." Tell them to make sure they fill their plates because you don't want anybody leaving hungry today. Ask a couple of individuals to share the details of their plates with the group.

_____

_____

_____

_____

_____

_____

_____

Commentary

We've all experienced the feeling of hunger. Maybe an early breakfast combined with a late lunch has left your stomach begging for a bagel. It's possible that an empty wallet or an absence of highway exits forced you to wait for French fries.

Personal Story

Tell the group about a time when you were really hungry. What were the circumstances? When did you finally get to eat? What did you eat? How did it taste?

_____

_____

_____

_____

_____

_____

Commentary

If you're like me, you've heard or read about "the feeding of the five thousand" nearly as many times as the number of people who were fed that day. But this time, one word gripped my attention like it never had before. It seems like a simple enough word, one that I have blown over time and time again. The word is buried at the beginning of verse 20—*satisfied.* Before now, the word didn't deserve much thought. How hard is it to understand that really hungry people ate a great deal of miraculous food and their tummies were filled? But this word got me thinking, "Were the people satisfied because they were full, or because they were in the presence of Jesus?" In Jesus, all of the prophetic teachings were fulfilled. He is the Alpha and the Omega, the beginning and the end. His power is made perfect in our weakness (2 Corinthians 12:9–10). Don't get me wrong; Scripture tells us that the people's stomachs were full. But the *souls* of the people were also being filled, with a salvation that comes only from the Savior. Today God fills us with His Word and the blessings that are ours in the Sacraments.

Concordance

Find one more verse that applies to this devotion. Possible key words include *Full, Filled,* and *Satisfied.* Or read:

From You comes my praise in the great congregation; my vows I will perform before those who fear Him. The afflicted shall eat and be satisfied; those who seek Him shall praise the LORD! May your hearts live forever! All the ends of the earth shall remember and turn to the LORD, and all the families of the nations shall worship before You. For kingship belongs to the LORD, and He rules over the nations (Psalm 22:25–28).

_____

_____

_____

_____

_____

_____

Meditate

Tell participants to listen closely to this final verse and meditate on its meaning. After a couple of moments, close with prayer.

Prayer Springboard

Jesus, thank You for satisfying our every need. You fill us up in every way through Your Word and Sacraments. Hear the praises of Your satisfied people as we say . . .

_____

_____

_____

_____

_____

_____

_____

20

Changing or Changeless?

Scripture Springboard

Do not be deceived, my beloved brothers. Every good gift and every perfect gift is from above, coming down from the Father of lights with whom there is no variation or shadow due to change. Of His own will He brought us forth by the word of truth, that we should be a kind of firstfruits of His creatures (James 1:16–18).

Activity

Ask two brave people to stand and act out a normal, everyday event. It could be as simple as talking to each other on the phone or shopping together at the grocery store. During their skit, another person has the power to call out, "Change!" This requires the person who just said the most recent line to begin his line again—but this time, he must communicate something different.

_____
_____
_____
_____
_____
_____
_____
_____
_____

Commentary

There is an old saying that goes, "Only two things are certain in life: death and taxes." We Christians know that this isn't true. Jesus is for certain. The Bible is certain.

Change is also inevitable. How many of you have changed your clothes since yesterday? Who has experienced a change in the weather in the last twenty-four hours? Yes, change is a major part of our everyday lives.

Personal Story

Tell the group about a change that you went through. Was it difficult? What was the outcome? Is the situation still changing?

_____
_____
_____
_____

_____
_____
_____
_____

able, and this mortal body must

put on immortality

(1 Corinthians 15:51–53).

_____
_____
_____
_____
_____
_____
_____

Commentary

From eight-tracks to cassettes to CDs. From rotary to touch-tone to cordless to cellular phones. Take a moment and think about the future. Could our familiar modes of transportation soon become a thing of the past? Could we one day be as comfortable with "Beam me up, Scotty" as Captain Kirk and Spock were?

No matter what the future brings, we can rely on the unchanging God of heaven and earth. We need never fear that God might change His mind and choose to stop loving us. There is no need to wonder if God will prefer a different means of salvation, other than the sacrificial death and resurrection of His Son, Jesus. God is not like the daily specials at our local diner, always changing. God is solid, firm, unmoving, and unchanging. He is always the same. It is comforting to know that God is in control of our future here on earth and for all eternity.

Meditate

Have participants listen to and then meditate upon the meaning of the verse you found. After a couple of moments, close with prayer.

Prayer Springboard

Dear Father of lights, we thank and praise You for being a firm foundation on which we can trust fully. . . .

_____
_____
_____
_____
_____
_____
_____

Concordance

Find one more verse that applies to this devotion. Possible key words include *Change*, *Tomorrow*, and *Firm*. Or read:

Behold! I tell you a mystery. We shall not all sleep, but we shall all be changed, in a moment, in the twinkling of an eye, at the last trumpet. For the trumpet will sound, and the dead will be raised imperishable, and we shall be changed. For this perishable body must put on the imperish-

21

A Great Ending

Scripture Springboard

Behold, I am coming soon, bringing My recompense with Me, to repay everyone for what he has done. I am the Alpha and the Omega, the first and the last, the beginning and the end (Revelation 22:12–13).

Activity

You will need several old magazines for this activity. Allow participants to work in pairs. Give each pair a magazine, scissors, glue sticks, and a sheet of blank paper. The teams will compete to see who can be first to find, cut out, and glue the entire alphabet, in order, onto their sheet of paper. You could award the winning team cans of alphabet soup. Hang all of the sheets on the wall for the group to admire.

_____

_____

_____

_____

_____

_____

_____

_____

Commentary

It's hard to finish things. You might find yourself running out of steam during a thirty-minute workout. Perhaps you lose interest in a thousand-piece puzzle. Have you ever fallen asleep during a movie?

Personal Story

Tell the group about a time when you didn't finish a project. What was the project? Why didn't you finish it? What happened to the unfinished project?

_____

_____

_____

_____

_____

_____

_____

Commentary

Think about all the things God finished. He created the universe and all that is in it in six days (Genesis 1:31–2:1). Jesus is the perfecter of our faith (Hebrews 12:2). Most important, Jesus boldly declared from the cross, "It is finished" (John 19:30).

In the last chapter of Revelation, Jesus declares, "I am the Alpha and the Omega, the first and the last, the beginning and the end" (Revelation 22:13). I can't help but wonder about what it will be like when Jesus comes again to take you and me home. Many books have been written and theories proclaimed, but God is the only one who knows that moment in time. Jesus said in Matthew 24:36, "But concerning that day and hour no one knows, not even the angels of heaven, nor the Son, but the Father only." For some people, not knowing how and when might cause fear concerning Jesus' second coming. As Christians we need not fear Christ's return. God's promise of salvation, given through His free gift of faith, is ours through Baptism. The Spirit reassures us of this great promise through God's Word and the Sacraments.

Concordance

Find one more verse that applies to this devotion. Possible key words include *Perfect, Return, Coming,* and *Finished.* Or read:

> *I appeal to you therefore, brothers, by the mercies of God, to present your bodies as a living sacrifice, holy and acceptable to God, which is your spiritual worship. Do not be conformed to this world, but be transformed by the renewal of your mind, that by testing you may discern what is the will of God, what is good and acceptable and perfect (Romans 12:1–2).*

Meditate

Listen closely to this final Bible verse and meditate on its meaning. After a couple of moments, close with prayer.

Prayer Springboard

Dear Jesus, through Your death on the cross and resurrection from the grave, we are complete in You. Thank You for handling all things perfectly, according to Your will. . . .

22

Suffering Well

Scripture Springboard

For this is a gracious thing, when, mindful of God, one endures sorrows while suffering unjustly. For what credit is it if, when you sin and are beaten for it, you endure? But if when you do good and suffer for it you endure, this is a gracious thing in the sight of God. For to this you have been called, because Christ also suffered for you, leaving you an example, so that you might follow in His steps (1 Peter 2:19–21).

Activity

Ask one person in the group to leave the room; he will be the "guesser." Choose one of the remaining participants to be the "winker." His job is to discreetly wink at the others in the room. When he does so, the person receiving the wink will sit down. Invite the "guesser" back into the room. Have everyone stand in a circle with the "guesser" in the center. As each person sits, the game pauses while the "guesser" tries to identify the "winker." The game continues until the "guesser" is correct. If the "guesser" thought you were the "winker" and you weren't, what was it like to be accused of doing something you didn't do?

_____

_____

_____

_____

_____

_____

_____

Commentary

How many of you have ever gotten in trouble for something you didn't do? Perhaps you were left "holding the bag" in school, at home, or at work. The punishment might have been severe, or perhaps it was a tap on the wrist. Regardless, it's no fun to suffer.

Personal Story

Tell the group about a time when you were falsely accused of doing something wrong. Did you suffer because of it? How did that make you feel?

_____

_____

_____

_____

_____

_____

_____

weak, then I am strong

(2 Corinthians 12:9–10).

Commentary

Take a moment to think about the suffering that Paul endured as he spread the Gospel message of Jesus. He was beaten, imprisoned, flogged, and shipwrecked; he suffered hunger and thirst; and he was almost killed by stoning. What did he do? He praised God and gave glory to Him (2 Corinthians 12:10). Every suffering Paul endured reminded him of Jesus.

Suffering unjustly is exactly what happened to Jesus. He didn't sin. We did. We deserved death on a cross. But He died instead. He suffered because of the wrong things you and I choose to do every day. Through Christ's glorious resurrection, He won eternal life for all who call on Him in faith. Like Paul, we praise Jesus, the Shepherd and Overseer of our souls (1 Peter 2:25).

Concordance

Find one or more verses that apply to this devotion. Possible key words include *Suffering*, *Persecution*, and *Pain*. Or read:

> *But He said to me, "My grace is sufficient for you, for My power is made perfect in weakness." Therefore I will boast all the more gladly of my weaknesses, so that the power of Christ may rest upon me. For the sake of Christ, then, I am content with weaknesses, insults, hardships, persecutions, and calamities. For when I am*

Meditate

Read and meditate on the verses that you found. After a couple of moments, close with prayer.

Prayer Springboard

Dear Lord, thank You for being our Savior. Help us to recall Your suffering during our times of suffering. . . .

_____

_____

_____

_____

_____

_____

_____

_____

23

Mirror Image

Scripture Springboard

Therefore be imitators of God, as beloved children. And walk in love, as Christ loved us and gave Himself up for us, a fragrant offering and sacrifice to God (Ephesians 5:1–2).

Activity

Have each participant choose a partner. Have partners stand facing each other, an arm's length apart. One person will start moving while the other tries to mirror his every motion. The hardest thing about this activity will be staying focused on the partner.

_____

_____

_____

_____

_____

_____

_____

Commentary

No matter how tall we grow, we will always look up to someone. The world is full of heroes, male and female. Maybe we admire them because they are physically amazing, like Olympic athletes or MVPs. Perhaps your hero stands head and shoulders above the rest because of his intellect or wisdom.

Personal Story

Tell the group about a person you admire. It might be a parent, teacher, or pastor. Why do you look up to him or her? Have you found yourself following his/her actions in your own life?

_____

_____

_____

_____

_____

_____

_____

Commentary

When we admire people so deeply, we often find ourselves trying to mirror their every move. We want to unveil the thing that makes them who they are, and then follow in their every footstep. Remember how difficult it was to actually look into the eyes of the person we mirrored earlier? When we look into our Savior's eyes, we see our sinful imperfection. Due to our sinfulness, we can never live up to God's standard.

Yet we also see in the eyes of our Savior His gracious welcome. In His Word, Christ invites us, "Come to Me, all who labor and are heavy laden, and I will give you rest. Take My yoke upon you, and learn from Me, for I am gentle and lowly in heart, and you will find rest for your souls. For My yoke is easy, and My burden is light" (Matthew 11:28–30). Through His gifts of body and blood, we receive forgiveness and the reassurance of life forever with Him.

Concordance

Find one more verse that applies to this devotion. Possible key words include *Imitate*, *Guide*, and *Eyes*. Or read:

> *And you, child, will be called the prophet of the Most High; for you will go before the Lord to prepare His ways, to give knowledge of salvation to His people in the forgiveness of their sins, because of the tender mercy of our God, whereby the Sunrise shall visit us from on high to give light to those who sit in darkness and in the shadow of death, to guide our feet into the way of peace (Luke 1:76–79).*

Meditate

Listen closely to this final verse and meditate on its meaning. After a couple of moments, close with prayer.

Prayer Springboard

Dear God, we praise and thank You for sending Jesus as our Savior from sin. By Your Word, keep us focused on You and Your will. . . .

24

Light in the Darkness

Scripture Springboard

The people dwelling in darkness have seen a great light, and for those dwelling in the region and shadow of death, on them a light has dawned (Matthew 4:16).

Activity

Give each person a sheet of paper, pen or pencil, and a blindfold. Ask them to tie the blindfolds over their eyes. When no one can see, pull out a basket of common, everyday household items. Ask the group not to talk during this activity. Give each person one item from the basket. Ask them to feel their item for five seconds, then pass it to their right. Continue until every person has touched and felt every item. Now, while still wearing their blindfolds, have each person write down as many items as they can remember.

Commentary

A dark place, completely devoid of light, can be uncomfortable, even scary. What a relief, what a comfort, when light floods the room again. Despite the immediate discomfort to the eyes, most of the people—if not all of them—welcome the light.

Personal Story

Tell the group a story about a time when you were left in the dark, either physically or mentally. How did that feel? What was it like to be in the light again?

----

darkness is as light with You

(Psalm 139:10–12).

_____

_____

_____

_____

_____

_____

Commentary

The one day of the year when I notice light the most is on Easter morning. The church's stained-glass windows seem brighter on that morning when a sliver of the rising sun shines through. Easter lilies lean toward the golden rays. The church colors are brighter—white and gold. The entire congregation feels new with recently purchased hats, dresses, and ties. The choir robes glimmer with a bit more pizzazz and the choir members beam winning smiles from ear to ear. Yet Easter isn't about any of these things. The real celebration on Easter morning is the risen Christ.

Even if Easter morning brings dark clouds and sheets of rain, even if the altar is stripped bare and the entire choir has called in sick, we can still celebrate, because "[the angel] said to them, 'Do not be alarmed. You seek Jesus of Nazareth, who was crucified. He has risen; He is not here. See the place where they laid Him'" (Mark 16:6). The joyous message of Easter, Christ's victory over sin, death, and the devil, is ours every day.

Concordance

Find one more verse that applies to this devotion. Possible key words include _Eyes_, _See_, and _Look_. Or read:

> _Even there Your hand shall lead_
> _me, and Your right hand shall_
> _hold me. If I say, "Surely the_
> _darkness shall cover me, and the_
> _light about me be night," even_
> _the darkness is not dark to You;_
> _the night is bright as the day, for_

Meditate

Listen closely to this final verse and meditate on its meaning. After a couple of moments, close with prayer.

Prayer Springboard

Dear risen Savior, we praise You for Your victory over sin, death, and the devil. Help us to joyfully celebrate this day and every day. Thank You for making us Your children through our Baptism. By Your Spirit, found in Your Word, strengthen us to live each day for You. . . .

_____

_____

_____

_____

_____

_____

25

Eat!

Scripture Springboard

Therefore do not be anxious, saying, "What shall we eat?" or "What shall we drink?" or "What shall we wear?" For the Gentiles seek after all these things, and your heavenly Father knows that you need them all. But seek first the kingdom of God and His righteousness, and all these things will be added to you (Matthew 6:31–33).

Activity

Before the group arrives, gather five plates, each holding a different snack, and aluminum foil to cover each plate. The snacks might include a chocolate morsel, a cookie, mini doughnuts, a gooey brownie, and a decadent chocolate bar. Make sure some snacks are "better" than others.

As people enter the room, give each person the same amount of play money. Tell them that you are going to conduct an auction during which they will bid on the individual plates of food. Only those with the winning bids will get a snack. They may eat it as soon as they purchase it.

Commentary

Food has never been as easy to obtain as it is today. Practically every corner in a busy city has a restaurant or store where you can easily purchase food. True hunger is a sensation that most Americans rarely experience.

Personal Story

Tell the group about a time when you were hungry. What kept you from eating? When you finally did eat, what did you eat? How did it taste?

Commentary

In today's society, when we find ourselves asking, "What will we eat and drink?" coming up with the answer is usually as simple as making a decision between a burger joint and a pizza place. We stand in our crammed closets for minutes, asking ourselves, "What will I wear?"

Today's Scripture reading asks these same questions, but from a different angle. These people didn't have food available at their fingertips. But Jesus instructed them (and us) to not worry about where the next morsel of food, sip of water, or stitch of clothes would come from. Jesus teaches us to worry about far more important things—God's kingdom.

Now, does this mean we will always have everything we desire? No! But God promises to provide all that we need—and what we need most is a Savior from sin. We are thankful that God has already provided this through His Son, Jesus Christ. God also blesses us with His Word, the Bible. As we spend time in the Word, we see the many other physical and spiritual blessings God grants us.

Concordance

Find an additional key verse that applies to this devotion. Possible key words include *Hunger*, *Thirst*, and *Clothe*. Or read:

Therefore they are before the throne of God, and serve Him day and night in His temple; and He who sits on the throne will shelter them with His presence. They shall hunger no more, neither thirst anymore; the sun shall not

strike them, nor any scorching heat. For the Lamb in the midst of the throne will be their Shepherd, and He will guide them to springs of living water, and God will wipe away every tear from their eyes (Revelation 7:15–17).

Meditate

Listen closely to this final verse and meditate on its meaning. After a couple of moments, close with prayer.

Prayer Springboard

Dear Father, thank You for all the blessings You give to us. Forgive us when we don't recognize Your hand of provision. Help us to seek first Your kingdom. . . .

26

Chosen People

Scripture Springboard

But you are a chosen people, a royal priesthood, a holy nation, a people belonging to God, that you may declare the praises of Him who called you out of darkness into His wonderful light (1 Peter 2:9 NIV).

Activity

Gather several different pictures of children displaying a variety of emotions. Give each person a moment to study the pictures and choose which child he most resembles at this moment. Then ask each person to choose one word that describes why he is like the child in the picture.

_____

_____

_____

_____

Commentary

All of us know the joy of being chosen and the disappointment of being cast aside. If we've ever been in the group when captains chose their teams, we might have been proud to be picked first, or ashamed to be selected last.

Personal Story

Tell the group about a time when you were chosen. Were you picked first? Were you picked last? Maybe you weren't selected for a job or task that you really wanted. What was that like?

_____

_____

_____

_____

_____

Commentary

I love walking into pet stores—and I hate it just as much. Nothing beats holding a brand-new puppy, cute and playful. In fact, if money were no object, I would purchase every pet in the place! But money *is* an object, and I usually put each puppy back into its cage and wander sadly back out the door. I imagine that each animal is somehow begging, "Please pick me!" I can almost see it in their eyes. I can almost hear their disappointment in their whimpers when I put them back. "Wait! What are you doing? I'm going home with you, aren't I? Don't put me back in here! Your car is out *there*!"

I'm thankful that I never need to feel that same disappointment on a spiritual level. Through Baptism, you and I have been chosen by God to be the people of God. What an honor and what a joy! Through Jesus Christ, the living Stone rejected by men and chosen by God, we too are living stones (1 Peter 2:5) being built into something bigger and better, the kingdom of God. Today's Scripture reading also reminds you and me that we were chosen so "that you may declare the praises of Him who called you out of darkness" (1 Peter 2:9). Why? So that others also might hear the Good News of Jesus Christ.

Concordance

Find one more verse that applies to this devotion. Possible key words include *Chosen*, *Stone*, and *Declare*.

I will extol You, my God and King, and bless Your name forever and ever. Every day I will bless You and praise Your name forever and ever. Great is the LORD, and greatly to be praised, and His greatness is unsearchable. One generation shall commend Your works to another, and shall declare Your mighty acts. On the glorious splendor of Your majesty, and on Your wondrous works, I will meditate. They shall speak of the might of Your awesome deeds,

and I will declare Your greatness. They shall pour forth the fame of Your abundant goodness and shall sing aloud of Your righteousness. The LORD is gracious and merciful, slow to anger and abounding in steadfast love. The LORD is good to all, and His mercy is over all that He has made (Psalm 145:1–9).

_____

_____

_____

_____

Meditate

Listen closely to this final verse and meditate on its meaning. After a couple of moments, close with prayer.

Prayer Springboard

Dear God, thank You for choosing us. It is a privilege to be Your children. Help us to share Your Word with others who have not yet heard. . . .

_____

_____

_____

_____

_____

_____

Date used

Used for

27

The Waiting Game

Scripture Springboard

It will be said on that day, "Behold, this is our God; we have waited for Him, that He might save us. This is the LORD; we have waited for Him; let us be glad and rejoice in His salvation" (Isaiah 25:9).

Activity

Challenge everyone to raise their hand at the precise moment a digital kitchen timer or stopwatch rings. First, set the timer for exactly one minute. Have every person close their eyes, and ask the group to be completely silent; no counting aloud, no tapping of feet or other signal. Then start the timer and say, "Go!" See how many can raise their hands at the exact moment the alarm goes off.

Commentary

Waiting is never easy. Yet we wait for things for a significant portion of our life. We wait for the light to turn green. We wait for the cookies to bake. We wait for our loved ones to return home. We wait in line at the drive-through. Waiting is inevitable.

Personal Story

Tell the group about a time when you had to wait for something. How long did you have to wait? What did you do to occupy your time while you were waiting?

Commentary

One thing the people in the Old Testament waited for was a Savior. Prophet after prophet spoke about the coming Messiah. While the people waited, they dreamed of what their champion would be like: strong, bold, aggressive, and powerful. No wonder they didn't recognize Jesus when He finally arrived. Their mighty Savior came in the form of a humble baby born in a stable. Take a look at His blood-line. Did I see a prostitute in there? Even though John the Baptizer declared His coming (Matthew 3:1–12), and God the Father announced His arrival (Matthew 3:13–17), still the people continued to watch and wait. Even Jesus' own disciples might have wondered, "When is this guy going to pick up a sword and lead us?" But Jesus wasn't that kind of leader. He led by compassion, gentleness, and humbleness.

Jesus displayed such great humility that He was obedient to the will of the Father and allowed Himself to be killed on a cross. Jesus' followers were no doubt frightened and disappointed when they saw Him die. They must have thought, "This is who we put our trust in? He died just like the rest of them!" Little did they know the champion they longed for was defeating death and the devil at that very moment. He would declare His victory three days later, on Easter morn.

We still wait today—not for a Savior, but for His second coming. We eagerly await the instant He returns and takes us to our heavenly home. It will be worth the wait.

and obtain the freedom of the glory of the children of God. For we know that the whole creation has been groaning together in the pains of childbirth until now. And not only the creation, but we ourselves, who have the firstfruits of the Spirit, groan inwardly as we wait eagerly for adoption as sons, the redemption of our bodies. For in this hope we were saved. Now hope that is seen is not hope. For who hopes for what he sees? But if we hope for what we do not see, we wait for it with patience (Romans 8:18–25).

_____

_____

_____

_____

Concordance

Find one more verse that applies to this devotion. Possible key words include *Wait* and *Patience*.

For I consider that the sufferings of this present time are not worth comparing with the glory that is to be revealed to us. For the creation waits with eager longing for the revealing of the sons of God. For the creation was subjected to futility, not willingly, but because of Him who subjected it, in hope that the creation itself will be set free from its bondage to decay

Meditate

Ask participants to listen closely to the verse you selected and meditate on its meaning. After a couple of moments, close with prayer.

Prayer Springboard

Dear Jesus, come quickly. Help us to be patient as You prepare a place for us with Yourself in heaven. . . .

_____

_____

_____

_____

28

Sheep Stuff

Scripture Springboard

*I am the good shepherd. I know
My own and My own know Me,
just as the Father knows Me and I
know the Father; and I lay down
My life for the sheep (John
10:14–15).*

Activity

Bring in a bag of apples, enough for every person to receive at least one. Give each person an apple and ask them to study it closely. After one minute, put all of the apples into a paper sack and mix them up. Then roll the apples onto the table and ask each person to select his apple from the bunch. Ask how they knew which apple was theirs. What did they look for?

_____

_____

_____

_____

_____

_____

Commentary

It can be very awkward going to a place where you don't know anybody. Imagine going to a party where you don't know a single person. It can be tough making friends, even acquaintances. The alternative is standing alone in a corner, watching the party pass you by.

Personal Story

Tell the group about a time when you went someplace where you didn't know anyone. What did that feel like? Did you eventually meet someone?

_____

_____

_____

_____

_____

_____

Commentary

For a Christian, one thing is true: no matter where you go or how alone you feel, God is always with you. David writes in Psalm 139:7–8, "Where shall I go from Your Spirit? Or where shall I flee from Your presence? If I ascend to heaven, You are there! If I make my bed in Sheol, You are there!"

God knows us intimately for three reasons: He created us; He saved us through the death and resurrection of His Son, Jesus; and He goes with us. Think about your nose and your ears; God formed them! Think about your feet and your hands. You guessed it! God intricately shaped them when you were in your "mother's womb" (Psalm 139:13). Consider your unique voice and incredible brain. Ponder how amazing just your heart is. Who else could have knit you together so perfectly, other than the God of the universe?

In our sin we wander away, leading to our downfall. But our loving Shepherd seeks us out and brings us back to Himself for all time. Through Baptism we are made part of His flock. What a comfort it is to know that we have Jesus Christ as our Good Shepherd and Savior. It is good to be in the presence of the Shepherd, safe and protected.

Concordance

Find one or more verses that apply to this devotion. Possible key words include *Shepherd*, *Sheep*, and *Know*. Or read:

Now may the God of peace who brought again from the dead our Lord Jesus, the great shepherd of the sheep, by the blood of the eternal covenant, equip you with everything good that you may do His will, working in us that which is pleasing in His sight, through Jesus Christ, to whom be glory forever and ever. Amen (Hebrews 13:20–21).

_____

_____

_____

_____

_____

_____

Meditate

Listen closely to the selected verses and meditate on their meaning. After a couple of moments, close with prayer.

Prayer Springboard

Dear Good Shepherd, thank You for making us Your precious sheep. Through Your Word, lead us through all the days of our life. . . .

_____

_____

_____

_____

_____

Date used
_____

Used for
_____

29

Great Command

Scripture Springboard

Hear, O Israel: The LORD our God, the LORD is one. You shall love the LORD your God with all your heart and with all your soul and with all your might. And these words that I command you today shall be on your heart. You shall teach them diligently to your children, and shall talk of them when you sit in your house, and when you walk by the way, and when you lie down, and when you rise. You shall bind them as a sign on your hand, and they shall be as frontlets between your eyes. You shall write them on the doorposts of your house and on your gates (Deuteronomy 6:4–9).

Activity

Give each person a 3 × 5 index card, a pen, and some tape. Repeat the following words until every person has written them on their card: "Love the LORD your God with all your heart and with all your soul and with all your might." Use push pins or tape to fasten each card around the doorframe of the room. Let them remain there for as long as you want.

_____
_____
_____
_____
_____

Commentary

As a family, what do you talk about when you are at home? Do you ever go for family walks? What do you discuss while you wander through your neighborhood? What is the first thing that you think about when you wake up? What is the last thing on your mind as you drift off to sleep?

Personal Story

Answer any of the questions listed above for the group. Invite volunteers to share their personal stories as well.

_____
_____
_____
_____
_____

Commentary

What an enormous challenge, to love the Lord with all of my heart, soul, and strength. It's not that I don't want to. It's just that I don't know how. So God gave the Israelites, and us, a four-step plan to make the impossible a reality: Teach, Talk, Tie, and Write.

Of course, this isn't the perfect recipe for a complete love for God; it's not even the start. Because of our sin we cannot even begin to love God. Rather, perfect love starts with God. 1 John 4:7–10 says:

> *Beloved, let us love one another,*
> *for love is from God, and whoever*
> *loves has been born of God and*
> *knows God. Anyone who does not*
> *love does not know God, because*
> *God is love. In this the love of*
> *God was made manifest among*
> *us, that God sent His only Son*
> *into the world, so that we might*
> *live through Him. In this is love,*
> *not that we have loved God but*
> *that He loved us and sent His Son*
> *to be the propitiation for our sins.*

Did you notice the order in this section of Scripture? God loved first. He demonstrated that love by sending Christ to save us from our sin so that we might live forever with Him in heaven. What wonderful news! The perfect love of God has nothing to do with me—and everything to do with Him.

Concordance

Find one more verse that applies to this devotion. Possible key words include *Heart*, *Soul*, *Strength*, and *Love*. Or read:

> *If the LORD had not been my help,*
> *my soul would soon have lived in*
> *the land of silence. When I*
> *thought, "My foot slips," Your*
> *steadfast love, O LORD, held me*

> *up. When the cares of my heart*
> *are many, Your consolations cheer*
> *my soul (Psalm 94:17–19).*

_____

_____

_____

_____

_____

Meditate

Listen closely to the final verse and meditate on its meaning. After a couple of moments, close with prayer.

Prayer Springboard

Dear Lord, we thank You for demonstrating Your love toward us through the death and resurrection of Jesus, our Savior. Strengthen our faith and love toward You as we partake of Your gift of Christ's body and blood given in the Sacrament of Holy Communion. . . .

_____

_____

_____

_____

30

Hear the Word

Scripture Springboard

Remember, then, what you received and heard. Keep it, and repent. If you will not wake up, I will come like a thief, and you will not know at what hour I will come against you (Revelation 3:3).

Activity

Invite participants to work in pairs to create a clever way to teach someone else how to tie the laces on their shoes. No bunnies jumping into their holes—that one's been done. Give teams a few minutes to brainstorm, and then ask for volunteers to teach their new method. Invite everyone to untie their shoes and follow along. If someone is wearing shoes without laces, have them borrow one with laces from a friend.

Commentary

The lessons we've learned from the day we were born are as countless as the fish in the sea. Some lessons are enjoyable, like learning to ride a bike, while others are not so fun, like learning long division or how to take out the trash.

Personal Story

Share with the group a particular lesson you remember learning. You may have enjoyed the lesson or disliked it. How do you use the lesson you learned back then today?

Commentary

We may learn something but then quickly forget what we've learned within a few days or even hours. Think about a student studying a foreign language. He might be able to pass a test on a given day, but ten years later, he might not remember a single word in that language. But what if that same student learned the language and then moved to a country where everyone speaks it? Not only would he *remember* the language, but it would become second nature to him. Why? Because the continuous practice would help him remember and use the words he learned.

How is this similar to our spiritual life? The Bible teaches truths that God intends for us to use in our daily lives. James 1:22–25 teaches us:

> *But be doers of the word, and not*
> *hearers only, deceiving yourselves.*
> *For if anyone is a hearer of the*
> *word and not a doer, he is like a*
> *man who looks intently at his*
> *natural face in a mirror. For he*
> *looks at himself and goes away*
> *and at once forgets what he was*
> *like. But the one who looks into*
> *the perfect law, the law of liberty,*
> *and perseveres, being no hearer*
> *who forgets but a doer who acts,*
> *he will be blessed in his doing.*

Through faith God strengthens us as we hear His Word, remember the Word, and live in His Word. God provides opportunities for us to gather regularly with others in worship and Bible study to be strengthened in our understanding of the Word. He also blesses us with pastors and Christian teachers to help us grow in our faith and life.

Concordance

Find one more verse that applies to this devotion. Possible key words include *Remember*, *Obey*, *Learn*, and *Lesson*. Or read:

> *Finally, brothers, whatever is true,*
> *whatever is honorable, whatever*
> *is just, whatever is pure, whatever*
> *is lovely, whatever is commend-*
> *able, if there is any excellence, if*
> *there is anything worthy of*
> *praise, think about these things.*
> *What you have learned and*
> *received and heard and seen in*
> *me—practice these things, and*
> *the God of peace will be with you*
> *(Philippians 4:8–9).*

_____

_____

_____

_____

_____

Meditate

Listen closely to the final verse and meditate on its meaning. After a couple of moments, close with prayer.

Prayer Springboard

Dear Lord, thank You for Your Holy Word. Through the power of Your Spirit, may it forever be on our hearts and minds. . . .

_____

_____

_____

_____

_____

31

Daydreams

Scripture Springboard

If then you have been raised with Christ, seek the things that are above, where Christ is, seated at the right hand of God. Set your minds on things that are above, not on things that are on earth (Colossians 3:1–2).

Activity

Obtain two or three boxes of large beverage straws. (They are readily available through warehouse clubs; or you might ask a local-fast food restaurant to donate straws for your group or church.) Divide participants into teams, and give the teams two to five minutes to connect the straws end to end. See whose freestanding "straw tower" reaches highest. (These creations can get quite tall!)

_____

_____

_____

_____

_____

_____

_____

Commentary

Has anyone ever accused you of having your head stuck in the clouds? I hope that no one has ever told you your mind was in the gutter! Perhaps a teacher caught you daydreaming when you should have been listening.

Personal Story

Tell the group about a daydream you frequently have. If someone were to catch you daydreaming, what would you be thinking about?

_____

_____

_____

_____

_____

_____

_____

Commentary

When our Scripture encourages us to "set your minds on things that are above," it is not talking about the clouds. Rather, Paul encourages us to think about heavenly things. In today's culture, we're obsessed with earthly matters. Current movies, music, and television demand our attention. Anger, rage, and filthy language consume our thoughts on a daily—even hourly—basis. Only God can perform a thorough "brainwashing" so that our minds can be set on things above.

Paul offers us one additional piece of advice in Colossians 3:17, where he writes, "Whatever you do, in word or deed, do everything in the name of the Lord Jesus, giving thanks to God the Father through Him." Now *that's* godly guidance. The next time you want to argue with your neighbor, do it all in the name of Jesus. It won't work. How about next time you want to spread lying gossip about a friend? Try doing *that* in the name of Jesus and check out your poor results.

Sadly, this side of heaven, we will never be able to completely resist these sins. But through His Word and the Sacraments, God promises to strengthen us to resist the temptations of this world.

Concordance

Find one more verse that applies to this devotion. Possible key words include *Minds*, *Above*, and *Thoughts*. Or read:

> *Therefore, preparing your minds for action, and being sober-minded, set your hope fully on the grace that will be brought to you at the revelation of Jesus Christ (1 Peter 1:13).*

Meditate

Ask participants to listen closely to this final verse and meditate on its meaning. After a couple of moments, close with prayer.

Prayer Springboard

Dear Lord, help us to heed Your Word for us. Strengthen us through Your blessed Sacraments to resist temptations the devil sends our way. . . .

32

Show Me the Money!

Scripture Springboard

Bring the full tithes into the storehouse, that there may be food in My house. And thereby put Me to the test, says the LORD of hosts, if I will not open the windows of heaven for you and pour down for you a blessing until there is no more need (Malachi 3:10).

Activity

Bring a fistful of coins for this object lesson. Ask everyone to dig into their pockets and place their loose change on the table and count it. Add up all the coins to find your grand total. Now, figure out what 10 percent of that amount would be. Finally, figure out what 11 percent and 12 percent would be. Set that amount aside.

Commentary

They say that money makes the world go round. In today's society, many are obsessed with the thought of money. "Where is the money?" "How can I get more?" Then they wonder, "What will I buy?" It's nearly impossible to turn on your television and not find a group of people trying to win a reality or game show to become the next millionaire.

Personal Story

If money were no object, what would you buy, and for whom? How much do you think that would cost? How much would 10 percent of that amount be? What would you do with your tithe? Which church, group, or organization would receive it? What would they do with your tithe to strengthen the kingdom of God?

Commentary

In Matthew 22:21, Jesus instructs the Pharisees, Herodians, and you and me to "render to Caesar the things that are Caesar's, and to God the things that are God's." In today's culture, we are easily persuaded to pay our taxes. We may not do it with a happy heart, but we know that the alternative can result in unwanted audits, fines, penalties, even jail time.

But God doesn't punish or imprison us when we don't give to the work of the Lord. He simply asks us to give "not reluctantly or under compulsion, for God loves a cheerful giver" (2 Corinthians 9:7). Do we tithe for God's sake or for ours? If no one gave another penny to the Church, would the kingdom of God still grow? If no one wrote another check, could the Holy Spirit still accomplish all of the things He desires? Yes! Then why do we tithe? In faith, we give God of our firstfruits in response to the many blessings He gives us. God invites us to support the work of His Church through our sacrificial gifts. Through the Church, God uses our financial gifts to help others hear His Word.

Concordance

Find one more verse that applies to this devotion. Possible key words include *Give, Taxes,* and *Generous.*

We want you to know, brothers, about the grace of God that has been given among the churches of Macedonia, for in a severe test of affliction, their abundance of joy and their extreme poverty have overflowed in a wealth of generosity on their part. For they gave according to their means, as I can testify, and beyond their means, of their own free will, beg-ging us earnestly for the favor of taking part in the relief of the saints—and this, not as we expected, but they gave themselves first to the Lord and then by the will of God to us (2 Corinthians 8:1–5).

_____

_____

_____

_____

_____

Meditate

Have participants listen closely to the verse you selected and meditate on its meaning. After a couple of moments, close with prayer.

Prayer Springboard

God, all that we have is already Yours. Help us to give generously with a joyful heart. Through Your Word, reveal to us the things You desire us to do with Your gifts. . . .

_____

_____

_____

_____

_____

Date used

Used for

33

Along the Way

Scripture Springboard

Keep steady my steps according to Your promise, and let no iniquity get dominion over me (Psalm 119:133).

Activity

Before the group arrives, collect a marker for each participant, and make photocopies of a blank map. On one map, plot out a trip with several turns and detours. When the participants arrive, give each one a marker and a blank map. For one minute, verbally describe the route you outlined on your map. Have them mark the identical path on theirs. Can they do it without your showing them your map? Take a minute to see who came closest—and who "got lost."

Commentary

In today's world of information and technology, it is difficult to get lost when traveling from point A to point B. Printable step-by-step directions and handheld GPS devices enable the average person to know exactly where he is, down to the tenth of a mile.

Personal Story

Tell the group about a time when you got lost. Where were you? How did you feel? How did you find your way to familiar territory? How long were you lost?

Commentary

Despite the fact that fewer and fewer people find themselves physically lost in today's age of technology, a staggering number of people are spiritually lost. People are searching for their direction in a variety of ways. Where the world offers psychics and palm readers, God offers His perfect Word, the Bible. Through His Spirit, God reveals the path to follow to those who open His Word and seek His will and direction for their lives. He may not tell you which job to take, whom to marry, or where you'll be living in five years, but God has made clear the final destination for all of those who believe in Him: heaven. Sin and Satan want to lead us down confusing detours along our journey toward heaven, but God made the path straight and clear, "Your word is a lamp to my feet and a light to my path" (Psalm 119:105).

Through faith in Jesus, sin has no rule over our lives. Jesus is and forever will be victorious over sin! God's Word, our life map, points us to our final and eternal destination: a home with Him in paradise. Along the way, God refuels us as we read and hear His Word and partake of the Lord's Supper. Enjoy the journey, because our trip's final stop has a scenic view beyond your imagination!

Concordance

Find one more verse that applies to this devotion. Possible key words include *Path*, *Guide*, *Lead*, and *Direct*. Or read:

> *And I will lead the blind in a way that they do not know, in paths that they have not known I will guide them. I will turn the darkness before them into light, the rough places into level ground. These are the things I do, and I do not forsake them (Isaiah 42:16).*

Meditate

Listen closely to this final verse and meditate on its meaning. After a couple of moments, close with prayer.

Prayer Springboard

Dear Jesus, lead us according to Your perfect path. Through Your Word, reveal to us the way You would have us to go. . . .

34

Giving It Your All

Scripture Springboard

Jesus looked up and saw the rich putting their gifts into the offering box, and He saw a poor widow put in two small copper coins. And He said, "Truly, I tell you, this poor widow has put in more than all of them. For they all contributed out of their abundance, but she out of her poverty put in all she had to live on"
(Luke 21:1–4).

Activity

Before the others arrive, hide a hundred pennies in the room where you meet. Give everyone one minute to find as many pennies as they can. Tell them that there will be an auction, and the more money they find, the more they can spend. After the minute of searching is over, say, "Before we start our auction, I'd like to give each of you a chance to tithe or give a gift to God from the money you found." Receive those pennies, then auction off a candy bar or bag of cookies. Finally, ask, "How would the auction have been different if you would have given every penny you found as a gift to God?"

Commentary

"What's in it for me?" "What did I win?" "What do I get out of it?" We're always looking for ways to pad our pockets or boost our bank accounts. We wander around, looking for the next penny in the parking lot or the next "get rich quick" scheme.

Personal Story

Tell the group about a time when you needed money. Did you ever find it? If you did, how did you spend it? If you didn't, how did God provide despite your lack of funds?

74

Commentary

Jesus looked up just in time to see the widow's generosity while He and His disciples were spending time at the temple. Imagine for a moment what the next chapter is in the life of this widow. Since she had no more money, can we assume that she probably starved, withered up into a tiny ball of flesh, and died? Or do you think that Jesus, who saw this woman's generosity with His own eyes, blessed her abundantly beyond her imagination?

While we don't know what really happened, God teaches us in His Word through His servant Paul, "The point is this: whoever sows sparingly will also reap sparingly, and whoever sows bountifully will also reap bountifully. Each one must give as he has made up his mind, not reluctantly or under compulsion, for God loves a cheerful giver" (2 Corinthians 9:6–7). I'm sure that the men who counted the temple treasury that day didn't even notice the widow's portion of the offering. Who notices two small coins that are worth so very little? But Jesus did. And Jesus noticed the widow's heart, which trusted completely in His care.

As we grow in our faith and understanding of God, He strengthens us through the study of His Word to trust in Him for all our needs. Like the widow, we can joyfully give of the gifts He has entrusted to us.

Concordance

Find one or more verses that apply to this devotion. Possible key words include *Gift*, *Give*, *Generous*, and *Offering*. Or read:

The wicked borrows but does not pay back, but the righteous is generous and gives; for those blessed by the LORD shall inherit the land, but those cursed by Him shall be cut off (Psalm 37:21–22).

Meditate

Listen closely to the selected verses and meditate on their meaning. After a couple of moments, close with prayer.

Prayer Springboard

Heavenly Father, thank You for providing all that we need in this body and life, especially for giving us Your Son, Jesus Christ, as our Savior from sin. Through Your Word, teach us to trust in Your generous hand to provide all that we need. . . .

35

As Busy as an Ant?

Scripture Springboard

Go to the ant, O sluggard; consider her ways, and be wise. Without having any chief, officer, or ruler, she prepares her bread in summer and gathers her food in harvest. How long will you lie there, O sluggard? When will you arise from your sleep (Proverbs 6:6–9)?

Activity

Pick a simple task, like building a tower with interlocking blocks. Divide the blocks evenly into two piles. Assign two people to one team and everyone else to a second team. Then direct each team to build a tower using all of their blocks. However, the team with only two people may work for only thirty seconds at a time, and then they must rest for fifteen seconds without touching their blocks. All of the people on the other team may continue to work nonstop. The first team to finish their tower wins.

Commentary

Imagine really wanting to work on an important project yet not having the time or ability to accomplish it. That can be very frustrating. What's even worse is when an important job or task needs to be accomplished, yet no one wants to do it. Has your mother ever said to you, "Your bedroom isn't going to clean itself!"?

Personal Story

Tell the group about a job that you hate to do. What do you hate about it? Do you eventually do the job? What could you do to make the job easier?

Commentary

Today's section of wisdom from Scripture tells us to observe the ant when we're feeling spiritually lazy. Consider what we know about ants. They are not hard to find. They usually are found in groups. The ant is typically on the move or hard at work. Ants work incredibly hard with one purpose only: to serve the queen ant. The slug, on the other hand, is usually quite difficult to find. It is typically found alone, crawling along at a snail's pace.

What lessons might we learn from the ant? Christians, like the ant, should be active in all the corners of the earth, carrying out the work of Christ. We can surround ourselves with fellow Christians for fellowship, support, and learning. We are granted numerous opportunities, as servants of Jesus Christ, to serve God's kingdom through our vocations.

Finally, we keep should keep our minds focused on serving only the King of kings. Too often it seems Christians are spiritual slugs. We sit in our padded pews and think to ourselves, "I sin and Jesus saves; good thing I'm forgiven!" We sing a few hymns and head for home, knowing that we'll do it all over again 167 hours from now. While it is true that we are justified from our sins through faith in Jesus Christ alone, life as a Christian includes so much more. In thanksgiving for the great gift of salvation, we should embrace those opportunities God gives us to serve Him and one another.

Concordance

Find one more verse that applies to this devotion. Possible key words include *Serve*, *Work*, *Labor*, and *Lazy*. Or read:

> *Come to Me, all who labor and are heavy laden, and I will give you rest. Take My yoke upon you, and learn from Me, for I am gentle and lowly in heart, and you will find rest for your souls (Matthew 11:28–29).*

_____

_____

_____

_____

_____

Meditate

Have participants listen to the verse you select and meditate on its meaning. After a couple of moments, close with prayer.

Prayer Springboard

Jesus, in joyous response to the gifts You give us, help us to serve You and work for Your kingdom. . . .

_____

_____

_____

_____

_____

36

Sheep, Coins, and Sons

Scripture Springboard

What man of you, having a hundred sheep, if he has lost one of them, does not leave the ninety-nine in the open country, and go after the one that is lost, until he finds it? And when he has found it, he lays it on his shoulders, rejoicing. And when he comes home, he calls together his friends and his neighbors, saying to them, "Rejoice with me, for I have found my sheep that was lost." Just so, I tell you, there will be more joy in heaven over one sinner who repents than over ninety-nine righteous persons who need no repentance (Luke 15:4–7).

Activity

Ask each person to find a partner. Each pair needs to designate a "sheep" and a "shepherd." Ask the shepherds to stand with their backs against a wall while putting a blindfold over their eyes. Ask the sheep to stand with their backs along the opposite wall but scrambled (not standing directly across from their partner). The goal is for the shepherds to move across the room and find their sheep while blindfolded. The shepherds can say or ask anything they need to, but the sheep can only make sheep sounds. Play until everyone has found their sheep.

Commentary

Most Christians read the parable of the ninety-nine sheep and think that the one lost sheep refers to those people who do not yet know Jesus Christ. To most Christians, this story is a healthy reminder that "We've gotta get out there and tell someone about Jesus!"

Personal Story

Tell the group about a friend or family member who doesn't know about Jesus. Have you ever tried to tell him about Jesus? What was the result?

Commentary

Verse 7 in this parable helps us understand that the parable of the lost sheep is also about you and me. Christians who already know Jesus as their Savior still sin. It is a daily, hourly, even minute-by-minute battle that you and I face as we choose sin over obedience to God. Satan makes sin look so inviting, so tantalizing, that we dive in headfirst. We bathe ourselves in the pleasure of sin, only to find ourselves, moments later, in the mud and the mire.

Think about another famous parable Jesus told, about the lost son. Sin seemed so fun—until he found himself sitting next to the pigs, begging for a bite from their buffet. It's at this point that the parable teaches us about repentance and sorrow over our sin. By the power of the Holy Spirit, given at our Baptism, we turn from sin and seek Christ's forgiveness. Immediately the heavenly party begins! Jesus also describes it this way in another of His "lost" parables: "Just so, I tell you, there is joy before the angels of God over one sinner who repents" (Luke 15:10).

Concordance

Find one more verse that applies to this devotion. Possible key words include *Repent*, *Forgiveness*, and *Sheep*. Or read:

> *And Jesus answered them, "Those who are well have no need of a physician, but those who are sick. I have not come to call the righteous but sinners to repentance"* (Luke 5:31–32).

_____

_____

_____

_____

Meditate

Listen closely to this final verse and meditate on its meaning. After a couple of moments, close with prayer.

Prayer Springboard

Perfect Shepherd, thank You for finding us in the muck of our sin and purchasing our forgiveness through Your suffering, death, and resurrection. Help us repent of those things that distract us from You. . . .

_____

_____

_____

_____

_____

_____

_____

37

Contentment

Scripture Springboard

Not that I am speaking of being in need, for I have learned in whatever situation I am to be content. I know how to be brought low, and I know how to abound. In any and every circumstance, I have learned the secret of facing plenty and hunger, abundance and need. I can do all things through Him who strengthens me (Philippians 4:11–13).

Activity

Borrow a large box of roofing nails from your neighborhood carpenter or handyman. Ask two people in the group, "Who is ready for a head-to-head challenge?" Tell the two challengers to pick up as many nails as they can in one handful. Obviously, the harder they try, the more discomfort they will experience while burying their hands in sharp nails. Count the number of nails each person grabbed and declare a winner.

Commentary

We constantly want more and more. Mentally walk through your local electronics store, and think about all of the things you'd buy if money were no object. A flat-screen television, surround-sound stereo, toys, trinkets, gadgets, and gizmos of all kinds would top a mile-long list for most of us.

Personal Story

Tell the group about the one thing that would top your "wish list." Why do you want that thing so much? How much does it cost? How would your life be different if you had it?

Commentary

Being content or satisfied is not a feeling many people experience in our culture. Commercials and billboards scream to us about the next new thing we must have. We fill our ever-growing stomachs with the next value meal or midday pizza buffet. I've recently realized that no matter how many pairs of shoes I have, I can still wear only one pair at a time.

The writer of the Letter to the Philippians, Paul, learned a very valuable lesson during his Gospel-spreading journeys: He learned to be content. No doubt there were times when his stomach rumbled with hunger, yet he chose to be content. I'm sure Paul's clothes grew tattered and his shoes wore thin, and yet he chose to be content. I'm positive that Paul didn't spend every night on a soft bed with a warm blanket. In fact, in 2 Corinthians 11:25, Paul tells us that for "a night and a day I was adrift at sea." And yet he found contentment in the promises of Christ. Paul knew contentment because through faith in Christ, he knew his final destination.

Consider Paul the next time you decide to be in a "got to have it" mood. What would Paul do? He'd encourage you to set your eyes on our Savior Jesus Christ and to be content in Him. He'd also tell you that you're going to need strength to overcome your earthly desires. Paul knows where to find that too; he tells us, "I can do all things through Him who strengthens me" (Philippians 4:13).

Concordance

Find one more verse that applies to this devotion. Possible key words include *Content*, *Satisfied*, *Desire*, and *Strength*. Or read:

Now there is great gain in godliness with contentment, for we brought nothing into the world, and we cannot take anything out of the world. But if we have food and clothing, with these we will be content (1 Timothy 6:6–8).

Meditate

Listen closely to this final verse and meditate on its meaning. After a couple of moments, close with prayer.

Prayer Springboard

Dear Jesus, give us the strength to be content and satisfied with all that You provide. Help us to seek Your kingdom rather than the things of this world. . . .

38

The Power of Prayer

Scripture Springboard

Now to Him who is able to do far more abundantly than all that we ask or think, according to the power at work within us, to Him be glory in the church and in Christ Jesus throughout all generations, forever and ever. Amen (Ephesians 3:20–21).

Activity

Ask the participants to go off by themselves and consider their most important prayer concern right now. Encourage them to pray specifically that God would handle their request in the way that is best for them. After a few minutes, ask the group to come back. Invite anyone who wants to to say one word that summarizes their request to God.

_____

_____

_____

_____

_____

_____

Commentary

Ask just about anyone you meet on the street, and you will find that they have a need of some kind. Maybe it's a need for food, clothing, shelter, or money. We can pretty much guarantee that *everyone* needs *something*.

Personal Story

Share your most fervent prayer or need with the group. How did you ask God to respond to your prayer? How would your life be different if God answered your request?

_____

_____

_____

_____

_____

Commentary

No matter what your prayer was a few minutes earlier, the way you would have God resolve it probably pales in comparison with the way He could or even desires to. He can do "far more abundantly than all we ask or imagine." Are you in need of a solid Christian friendship? God can provide immeasurably more! Do you need a special measure of good health? God can provide immeasurably more! Do you need unique guidance or instructions from an all-knowing, ever-present God? He can provide immeasurably more! Are you in need of a love that knows no limitations or boundaries? God can provide immeasurably more! Do you need renewal for a broken family? God can provide immeasurably more!

Does that mean that He always will? No. We know that God can accomplish all things, but He often replies "No" or "Wait" to our prayer because His timing and will are better for us, even when we don't see that or understand it. So have faith in these two things: God can answer your prayer far beyond your wildest imagination, and when He says "No" or "Wait," it is because His perfect timing and will are better than ours.

Concordance

Find two additional verses that apply to this devotion. Possible key words include *Prayer*, *Imagine*, and *Provide*. Or read:

> *None of the rulers of this age understood this, for if they had, they would not have crucified the Lord of glory. But, as it is written, "What no eye has seen, nor ear heard, nor the heart of man imagined, what God has pre-pared for those who love Him"— these things God has revealed to us through the Spirit. For the Spirit searches everything, even the depths of God (1 Corinthians 2:8–10).*

Meditate

Encourage participants to listen to and meditate on the meaning of your selected verses. After a couple of moments, close with prayer.

Prayer Springboard

Send the group back to their original loca-tions for a few minutes, and encourage them to pray one more time, asking God to answer their prayer in the way and at the time He wills. . . .

39

Face-to-Face

Scripture Springboard

And now, little children, abide in Him, so that when He appears we may have confidence and not shrink from Him in shame at His coming (1 John 2:28).

Activity

Grab a set of trivia cards and divide the group into boys and girls. Ask the girls a question. If they get it right, they receive one million points. If they get it wrong, the boys can steal the points by answering the question correctly. The team with the most points at the end of a few minutes wins.

Commentary

I wonder, for a moment, what it would be like to be all-knowing, omniscient. Going to school would seem like a waste of time; you would already know all of the answers! You could be a worldwide celebrity and multibillionaire because you would post perfect winning streaks on the game shows of your choice.

Personal Story

Can you think of other ways in which your life would be different if you were all-knowing? To what burning questions would you finally know the answers? Is there any question to which you would rather *not* know the answer?

Commentary

The triune God, of course, is the only one who ever is and ever will be omniscient. Our heavenly Father is the only one who knows when He is returning to earth to take us to be with Him in heaven (Mark 13:32–37). Sometimes when I think about God's return, I become nervous. I think to myself, "You mean the perfect

God who knows everything about me will come to earth and I will see Him face-to-face?" I suddenly feel ashamed because I can make a mile-long list of the things I've done wrong. I worry that my sins will be too numerous and God might pass me by.

But John puts Satan's lies to rest when he reminds us that we can be confident and unashamed when Christ comes back. How is that possible? First, through Christ, we are forgiven, redeemed, and made pure, through His death on the cross and His glorious resurrection on Easter morning. Psalm 103:12 reminds us that "as far as the east is from the west, so far does He remove our transgressions from us." There is no doubt; we have been justified through Jesus.

Finally, John encourages us to live a sanctified life when he instructs us to "abide in Him" (2:28). We can turn our faces toward the sky and welcome the return of Jesus. We long for His triumphant return with confidence and are not ashamed.

Concordance

Find one more Bible verse that applies to this devotion. Possible key words include *Justified*, *Return*, *Unashamed*, and *Confident*. Or read:

For by works of the law no human being will be justified in His sight, since through the law comes knowledge of sin. But now the righteousness of God has been manifested apart from the law, although the Law and the Prophets bear witness to it—the righteousness of God through faith in Jesus Christ for all who believe. For there is no distinction: for all have sinned and fall short of the glory of God, and are justified by His grace as a gift,

through the redemption that is in Christ Jesus, whom God put forward as a propitiation by His blood, to be received by faith. This was to show God's righteousness, because in His divine forbearance He had passed over former sins. It was to show His righteousness at the present time, so that He might be just and the justifier of the one who has faith in Jesus. Then what becomes of our boasting? It is excluded. By what kind of law? By a law of works? No, but by the law of faith. For we hold that one is justified by faith apart from works of the law (Romans 3:20–28).

Meditate

Have participants listen closely to this final verse and meditate on its meaning. After a couple of moments, close with prayer.

Prayer Springboard

Come quickly, Lord Jesus, come quickly. We long to see You face-to-face so that we may come into our heavenly home. . . .

85

40

Good News for Bad News

Scripture Springboard

In My Father's house are many rooms. If it were not so, would I have told you that I go to prepare a place for you? And if I go and prepare a place for you, I will come again and will take you to Myself, that where I am you may be also. And you know the way to where I am going (John 14:2–4).

Activity

Give everyone a 3 × 5 note card and instruct the participants to make a Pastor Appreciation Card for your congregation's pastor. Tell them to draw a picture on one side and write some affirming words on the other. After a few minutes, collect all the cards and immediately toss them into the nearest trash can. (Make sure to put a clean trash bag in the empty can before everyone gets there.)

_____

_____

_____

_____

_____

_____

Commentary

Imagine the following scenario: Your favorite cousin is driving to your home for an overnight visit on his way to a distant destination. Overwhelmed by excitement, you make up a bed, cook an amazing dinner, and clean every square inch of the bathroom. Moments before you're expecting your cousin, he calls and tells you he has changed his plans; he won't be coming by after all. How disappointing!

Personal Story

Have you ever prepared something for someone and he never got to see it or experience it? What was it? How did that feel?

_____

_____

_____

_____

_____

Commentary

Do you want the good news first or the bad news? The Good News is that Jesus is preparing a place for us in heaven! I know that because He tells us so in John 14. Try to imagine for a moment what heaven will be like. While our limited human minds will never fully understand or comprehend what our Father's house will be like, we know that Jesus is coming back for all who believe in Him. Jesus wouldn't prepare a perfect place for us if He never intended to return and take us home with Him. Furthermore, we know that our Father's house has many rooms. Our loved ones who believed in Jesus and have passed away could be in a room just down the hall from ours. I don't know about you, but I can't wait for heaven!

But that's the bad news: we do have to wait. No one knows the time or day when Jesus will come back to earth to take us home. So until then, we have to wait. But we don't wait idly, watching the sky for our returning King. This is our chance to help others learn about Jesus so that they can believe in Him and experience heaven for all eternity.

So, go ahead; long for heaven. There's nothing wrong with longing. But in the meantime, pray that God would give us opportunities to share His saving Word with others.

Concordance

Find one more verse that applies to this devotion. Possible key words include *Promise*, *Paradise*, and *Heaven*. Or read:

He who has an ear, let him hear what the Spirit says to the churches. To the one who conquers I will grant to eat of the tree of life, which is in the paradise of God (Revelation 2:7).

Meditate

Listen closely to this final verse and meditate on its meaning. After a couple of moments, close with prayer.

Prayer Springboard

Dear Jesus, thank You for preparing a heavenly place for us. We thank You for Your death on the cross and resurrection from the grave so that we may defeat death and experience eternity with You. . . .

41

No Worries

Scripture Springboard

No, in all these things we are more than conquerors through Him who loved us. For I am sure that neither death nor life, nor angels nor rulers, nor things present nor things to come, nor powers, nor height nor depth, nor anything else in all creation, will be able to separate us from the love of God in Christ Jesus our Lord (Romans 8:37–39).

Activity

Play a rough-and-tumble game of "Taffy Pull." One person sits on the floor while the rest of the group grabs on to that person as tightly as possible. As the leader of the group, your task is to pull one person from the taffy cluster. Once that person is free, he also becomes a "taffy puller." Continue until only one person is left clinging to the original "piece of taffy." That person is declared the winner. Obviously, this is not a game you would play on Sunday morning.

_____
_____
_____
_____
_____

Commentary

The devil is constantly on the attack. The defeated one always tried another tactic to affect our relationship with Jesus in a negative way. 1 Peter 5:8 says, "Be sober-minded; be watchful. Your adversary the devil prowls around like a roaring lion, seeking someone to devour."

Personal Story

Tell the group about a time when you felt the devil prowling around you. How did God protect you? How did God use His Word and Sacraments to rescue you?

_____
_____
_____
_____
_____
_____
_____

Commentary

There is nothing more that the devil wants for us than to be actually separated, or at least *feel* separated, from Jesus Christ. The devil delights in those who have no connection to Jesus Christ. These people wander around the world denying their need for a Savior. These individuals are no longer on the devil's "to do" list.

Satan concentrates his greatest efforts on Christians, like you and me. He uses tools like trouble, hardship, persecution, famine, nakedness, danger, and the sword to try to separate us from our Savior (Romans 8:35). But just as the devil's gnarled hand reaches for another tool of destruction and separation, Jesus reminds us to get dressed and ready for battle. Jesus prepares us to be "more than conquerors" because of Him who first loved us. No doubt the battle is fierce, but Jesus has a grip on us and will not let us go under any circumstances. Christ will not allow us to be separated from Himself. The devil may try, but he always fails. In the grip of Jesus' nail-pierced hands alone there is eternal victory.

Concordance

Find one more verse that applies to this devotion. Possible key words include *Separate*, *Grasp*, and *Hold*. Or read:

> *"And I will make you to this people a fortified wall of bronze; they will fight against you, but they shall not prevail over you, for I am with you to save you and deliver you," declares the LORD. "I will deliver you out of the hand of the wicked, and redeem you from the grasp of the ruthless"* *(Jeremiah 15:20–21).*

Meditate

Have participants listen closely to this final verse and meditate on its meaning. After a couple of moments, close with prayer.

Prayer Springboard

Jesus, Your mighty grip is evident in our lives. Through Your powerful Word and strengthening Sacraments, continue to be our great defender. By Your mighty hand, protect us from the evil schemes of the devil. . . .

42

Wiped Clean

Scripture Springboard

If we say we have no sin, we deceive ourselves, and the truth is not in us. If we confess our sins, He is faithful and just to forgive us our sins and to cleanse us from all unrighteousness (1 John 1:8–9).

Activity

Give every person a page from a newspaper. Tell them to crumple the newspaper into a ball and smear as much printing ink onto their hands as possible. Give them a moment to look at their hands and consider the sin in their own lives. Next, give each person a baby wipe to wash their hands clean. Finally, instruct each person to lay out the wipe neatly in front of them, and as they look at it, consider how Jesus took our sins upon Himself.

Commentary

In Psalm 69:14, David wrote, "Deliver me from sinking in the mire; let me be delivered from my enemies and from the deep waters." Have you ever felt this way, trapped by the muck and the mire of sin?

Personal Story

Share with the group a time when God rescued you from the mire of sin. Remember that you don't want this story to be about you; rather, it should focus on the saving nature of Jesus Christ. Your story can be as simple as an account of your Baptism.

Commentary

Mud spreads quickly. Watch a small child who has touched some mud; before long, his body will be covered in gooey brown from head to toe. Sin is much the same way. We think to ourselves that it will only be for a moment; "I'll only take a peek"; "I'll try it just this one time." Then, before we know it, we've fallen into the deep hole that we ourselves have dug. Psalm 7:15 describes it like this: "He makes a pit, digging it out, and falls into the hole that he has made." We stand in a hole of sin, and it is far too deep for us to get out. We strain our neck looking upward while waiting for a rescuer. Oh, sure, we *try* to get out on our own. We test the walls to see if we can get a foothold; but we only slide to the bottom and become reacquainted with the muck we're trying to avoid.

Then Jesus comes. Whether He reaches in or jumps in and lifts us out, either way, we're free, and Jesus has taken on the burden of our sin. 2 Corinthians 5:21 says, "For our sake He made Him to be sin who knew no sin, so that in Him we might become the righteousness of God."

Did you hear what God's Word said? It didn't say that we jumped back into sin because we know Jesus will eventually come along and save us again. No, it said, "we become the righteousness of God." Empowered by the Holy Spirit as we study God's Word and partake of the Lord's Supper, we strive to live a righteous life, a life without sin.

Concordance

Find one more verse that applies to this devotion. Possible key words include *Sin, Cleanse, Forgiveness,* and *Purify.* Or read:

Submit yourselves therefore to God. Resist the devil, and he will flee from you. Draw near to God, and He will draw near to you.

Cleanse your hands, you sinners, and purify your hearts, you double-minded. Be wretched and mourn and weep. Let your laughter be turned to mourning and your joy to gloom (James 4:7–9).

_____

_____

_____

_____

_____

Meditate

Listen closely to this final verse and meditate on its meaning. After a couple of moments, close with prayer.

Prayer Springboard

Dear Jesus, thank You for saving us from our sin. We needed a Savior, and You heard our cry. We are forever thankful, for You alone could rescue us. . . .

_____

_____

_____

_____

_____

43

A Little Light

Scripture Springboard

Your word is a lamp to my feet and a light to my path (Psalm 119:105).

Activity

For this activity you'll need a small ladder or a tall person standing on a chair. Ask everyone to gather around the ladder or chair while giving the elevated person a flashlight. Turn off all the lights. The challenge is for each person in the room to be within the flashlight's beam. At first, hold the flashlight high so that it casts a wide beam; it will be easy for everyone to find a spot in the light. But slowly, very slowly, the flashlight should be lowered until eventually it hovers just an inch from the floor. Can your entire group get any part of their body in the light?

Commentary

We all know the value of being in God's Word on a regular, even daily, basis. Daily instructions from God can only enable us to live a more balanced, joy-filled life. The question, then, is why do so few Christians find time in their day to sit at the feet of Jesus by studying the Bible?

Personal Story

Tell the group about a time when you were regularly in God's Word. Compare that to times when you haven't chosen to study the Bible. How was life different for you? What changes did you notice?

Commentary

Today's Scripture verse tells us that God's Word will light our path. Imagine walking down a forest trail in the middle of the night. The dense forest canopy blocks out any light the night's thin sliver of moon provides. You can barely see your hand in front of your face. Then you remember your flashlight, hidden away in the depths of your backpack. You say a quick prayer, "Please let the batteries still be good." You click on your flashlight and welcome the flood of light that illuminates your path. Finally, you can see.

Now what? The assumption is that you will walk. The theory is that when your path is well lit, you will put one foot in front of the other.

Jonah didn't. God cast a light on Jonah's path when He commanded, "Arise, go to Nineveh, that great city, and call out against it, for their evil has come up before Me" (Jonah 1:2). The floodlight of God's voice lit the desired path for Jonah, and yet he ran in the opposite direction.

We are sometimes like Jonah. We ask God to light our paths, to make our future clear, and then when He does, we run in the opposite way because "that isn't the way I would have done it, Lord." Fortunately for Jonah, God gave him another chance, and this time Jonah listened to God's voice and shared His message of repentance with the people of Nineveh. We can thank God that He gives us another chance too—over and over again. Through the suffering and death of Jesus, and His glorious resurrection, we receive forgiveness, life, and eternal salvation.

Concordance

Find one or more Bible verses that apply to this devotion. Possible key words include *Light, Lamp,* and *Obedience.* Or read:

Now to Him who is able to strengthen you according to my gospel and the preaching of Jesus Christ, according to the revelation of the mystery that was kept secret for long ages but has now been disclosed and through the prophetic writings has been made known to all nations, according to the command of the eternal God, to bring about the obedience of faith—to the only wise God be glory forevermore through Jesus Christ! Amen (Romans 16:25–27).

Meditate

Ask participants to listen closely to the verses you selected and meditate on their meaning. After a couple of moments, close with prayer.

Prayer Springboard

God, the eternal Source of light, shed light on our path through Your Word. Show us the direction You would have us go. By Your Spirit working through Your Word, strengthen us to be obedient to Your guiding. . . .

Date used

Used for

44

Freely Forgiven

Scripture Springboard

For if you forgive others their trespasses, your heavenly Father will also forgive you, but if you do not forgive others their trespasses, neither will your Father forgive your trespasses (Matthew 6:14–15).

Activity

Ask the group to stand in a circle. Give each person something heavy. Ask everyone to close their eyes and bow their heads. Quietly walk around the outside of the circle and tap one person on the head. That person will be the only one allowed to forgive. Once you have made your selection, have everyone open their eyes and wander around the room, asking, "Will you forgive me?" Only the selected person may answer "yes"; everyone else is instructed to say "no." Once they've found the person who will forgive them, participants should set their heavy items on the nearest table. Play until only one person is still carrying his heavy burden.

Commentary

Being forgiven is one of the greatest feelings a person can experience. Perhaps you've hurt a loved one, and now you feel as bad, if not worse, than they do. You didn't mean to hurt him, but you did.

Personal Story

Tell about a time when you inadvertently hurt a loved one. How did that feel? How did you ask for forgiveness? Was it granted? How did being forgiven feel?

Commentary

Being forgiven is like having the weight of the world suddenly lifted off your sagging shoulders. You can finally breathe deeply again because the hurt you caused and felt has melted away. The very forgiveness that Jesus earned for us has prevailed again!

Imagine what life would be like if we refused to forgive. Grudges would take hold and wars waged. Within days, maybe even hours, our world would be littered with beaten people seeking only revenge. Maybe this sounds scary to you. Maybe this sounds like a slice of your family's reality. Either way, this was not God's plan for our lives on this earth. God clearly outlined His plan for us in Colossians 3:13 when, through the apostle Paul, He says, "Bear with each other and forgive whatever grievances you may have against one another. Forgive as the Lord forgave you" (NIV). Step one was God's perfect model of forgiveness. He gave His one and only beaten and bloodied Son as its very symbol. Since God freely gave His Son, Jesus, as our Savior from sin, death, and the devil, we can forgive one another for the hurtful comment, the nasty note, the spiteful action. It is tough to forgive those who wrong and harm us, but through His Word and Sacraments, God strengthens us to forgive as He forgave.

Concordance

Find one more verse that applies to this devotion. Possible key words include *Absolution*, *Forgive*, *Forgiven*, and *Forgiveness*. Or read:

> *And whoever speaks a word against the Son of Man will be forgiven, but whoever speaks against the Holy Spirit will not be forgiven, either in this age or in the age to come (Matthew 12:32).*

Meditate

Ask participants to listen closely to this final verse and meditate on its meaning. After a couple of moments, close with prayer.

Prayer Springboard

Dear Father, help us to forgive just as You have forgiven us. . . .

Date used

Used for

45

Here's Heaven

Scripture Springboard

For the Lord Himself will descend from heaven with a cry of command, with the voice of an archangel, and with the sound of the trumpet of God. And the dead in Christ will rise first. Then we who are alive, who are left, will be caught up together with them in the clouds to meet the Lord in the air, and so we will always be with the Lord (1 Thessalonians 4:16–17).

Activity

Art time! Pass out sheets of paper and crayons, markers, or colored pencils. Give each person four minutes to draw his vision of what heaven will be like. Allow one minute for show-and-tell.

_____
_____
_____
_____
_____
_____
_____
_____
_____

Commentary

Nobody knows what heaven will be like. People have tried to guess: streets of gold, mansions, all-you-can-eat buffets. But heaven, for the most part, remains an eagerly anticipated mystery.

Personal Story

Show the group your drawing of heaven. On what knowledge did you base your picture? How has your image of heaven changed from when you were a child?

_____
_____
_____
_____
_____
_____
_____
_____

Commentary

As if dissecting heaven isn't hard enough, everyone seems to wonder what Christ's second coming will be like too. "Will I fly toward heaven?" "Will I ride on a cloud?" "Will I still be married in heaven?" "Will I recognize loved ones?" "Will I be thinner?" "How long *is* eternity, anyway?"

Brace yourself, because I have the answer to all of these questions and more: it doesn't matter. Here's what you need to know about Christ's triumphant return and life eternal: it's all about Jesus! Heaven is not about you, your fourteen-bedroom condo on the beach of paradise's shore, or even your million-mile-a-gallon cloud. Jesus is the center and focus of heaven, and our truest reward is to praise and worship Him for all eternity. We were created for this very reason, to give glory and honor to God forever and ever. Yes, the accommodations will be unbelievable, beyond our wildest imagination, but they will pale in comparison with seeing the almighty Jesus face-to-face, day after glorious day.

Concordance

Find one or more verses that apply to this devotion. Possible key words include *Heaven*, *Return*, and *Eternity*. Or read:

> *But grow in the grace and knowledge of our Lord and Savior Jesus Christ. To Him be the glory both now and to the day of eternity. Amen (2 Peter 3:18).*

Meditate

Listen closely to the final verses and meditate on their meaning. After a couple of moments, close with prayer.

Prayer Springboard

Jesus, precious Savior, thank You for our promised inheritance of heaven, which You earned for us upon the cross of Calvary. Our souls long to worship and praise You forevermore. . . .

46

Sowing Seeds

Scripture Springboard

And He said to them, "The harvest is plentiful, but the laborers are few. Therefore pray earnestly to the Lord of the harvest to send out laborers into His harvest. Go your way; behold, I am sending you out as lambs in the midst of wolves" (Luke 10:2–3).

Activity

You'll need a stack of foam cups, dirt or potting soil, a variety of seeds, and some water. Explain to the group that they are going to plant a mini garden. Each person can choose what he want to plant. When the seeds are sown, sprinkle with some water and wait for growth (in a few weeks, of course).

Commentary

I despise gardening! The combination of bending over, an aching back, muddy hands, and a sweaty brow keeps me longing for a cheeseburger, French fries, and a chocolate milk shake. Truth be told, I don't even enjoy vegetables (but please don't tell my children that).

Personal Story

Do you enjoy gardening? Why or why not? As a child, did you ever tend your parents' garden? What was that like?

Commentary

Fortunately, the type of gardening to which Jesus calls us in Luke 10:2 is meant to bring joy during our Christian walk of faith. Jesus' comment is motivated by the view He sees when He gazes longingly upon field after field after field of unfaithful people. God yearns to spend eternity with all of His created people, including the friends and family close to you who do not know Him as Lord and Savior. No doubt you've longed for them to become faithful believers in Jesus Christ. But have you ever prayed that God would use you as the laborer? Jesus even instructs you and me to ask, pray, even *plead* to be His tool to introduce people to Him. This thought seems scary to many Christians, so much so that some of us will never know the challenges and joys of sharing the Gospel message with a loved one. Through the time you spend in His Word, God prepares you to go out as a laborer to gather those whom He has made ripe for harvest.

Concordance

Find one more verse that applies to this devotion. Possible key words include *Harvest*, *Proclaim*, and *Labor*. Or read:

> *For I long to see you, that I may impart to you some spiritual gift to strengthen you—that is, that we may be mutually encouraged by each other's faith, both yours and mine. I want you to know, brothers, that I have often intended to come to you (but thus far have been prevented), in order that I may reap some harvest among you as well as among the rest of the Gentiles (Romans 1:11–13).*

——————————————————
——————————————————
——————————————————
——————————————————
——————————————————

Meditate

Listen closely to this final verse and meditate on its meaning. After a couple of moments, close with prayer.

Prayer Springboard

Lord of the harvest, please use us as You will to tell others about You. Through Your Word, strengthen and prepare us for service in our world. . . .

——————————————————
——————————————————
——————————————————
——————————————————
——————————————————
——————————————————
——————————————————
——————————————————
——————————————————
——————————————————
——————————————————
——————————————————

47

Life-Giving Connection

Scripture Springboard

Abide in Me, and I in you. As the branch cannot bear fruit by itself, unless it abides in the vine, neither can you, unless you abide in Me. I am the vine; you are the branches. Whoever abides in Me and I in him, he it is that bears much fruit, for apart from Me you can do nothing (John 15:4–5).

Activity

Have participants stand side by side at one end of the room. Connect them into one long line by having them hold the ends of two 3-foot-long paper party streamers, one in each hand. Then have them run from one side of the room to the other while keeping their streamers intact. If one of their streamers tears, they can continue to run. But if both streamers get torn, they must sit down at the exact spot where they became disconnected. Many streamers will break naturally, but your job as the leader in this game is to break as many streamers as possible.

Commentary

Imagine a person who is very near death, lying in a hospital bed. Odds are he is connected to several machines. One tube provides oxygen; another provides nourishment; and still another tube provides fluids. Disconnect these tubes, or even one of them, and the person will probably die—just wither away.

Personal Story

Have you ever had a friend or loved one in a hospital? What tubes were they connected to? What did that look like to you? Have you ever been the one in the hospital connected to tubes? What was that like?

Commentary

It's no surprise that as Christians, our desire is to be connected to Christ. We know that without Christ, we can do nothing. We recognize that if we were to venture out into life alone, without Christ, we would begin to self-destruct as soon as we became disconnected from Him. Therefore, we remain connected to Jesus in Word and Sacrament so that we might bear fruit.

Then what? Too often we display our fruit on the vine and boast, "Look at my fruit. Doesn't it look yummy?" Using our fruit to serve others rarely comes to mind. We are content simply to hold on to our fruit as tightly as we try to hold on to Jesus.

In the part of the world where I live (maybe yours too), fruit that is never picked off the tree or the vine eventually falls off and rots. So if we must remain in Jesus so that we can produce good fruit, it must be assumed that we are to use that fruit to serve others. Through His Spirit, as we stay connected to the Word, God empowers us to use the fruit that He has given us to benefit others. What fruit have been produced in your life because you are connected to Jesus? Whatever the fruit, share it with others so that they might taste the goodness of God through you.

Concordance

Find one more verse that applies to this devotion. Possible key words include *Fruit, Remain, Vine,* and *Branches.* Or read:

> *Likewise, my brothers, you also have died to the law through the body of Christ, so that you may belong to another, to Him who has been raised from the dead, in order that we may bear fruit for God. For while we were living in the flesh, our sinful passions, aroused by the law, were at work in our members to bear fruit for death. But now we are released from the law, having died to that which held us captive, so that we serve not under the old written code but in the new life of the Spirit (Romans 7:4–6).*

_____

_____

_____

_____

_____

_____

Meditate

Listen closely to this final verse and meditate on its meaning. After a couple of moments, close with prayer.

Prayer Springboard

Dear Jesus, thank You for remaining in us so that we can remain in You. Help us produce good fruit to serve others. . . .

_____

_____

_____

_____

_____

_____

_____

48

I Just Wanna Be a Sheep

Scripture Springboard

Before Him will be gathered all the nations, and He will separate people one from another as a shepherd separates the sheep from the goats. And He will place the sheep on His right, but the goats on the left. Then the King will say to those on His right, "Come, you who are blessed by My Father, inherit the kingdom prepared for you from the foundation of the world" (Matthew 25:32–34).

Activity

Give each person a small, snack-size bag of your favorite colored candy. Explain that the first person to open his bag, empty the contents, and sort the candies into piles by color will be declared the winner. Of course, after the winner is declared, eat up.

Commentary

Sheep are dumb! In fact, they are so dumb that they will eat an entire field of grass and then look at the ground and wonder where all of the grass went. It's a good thing that sheep have a shepherd to make them "lie down in green pastures" (Psalm 23:2).

Personal Story

Did you ever do anything really dumb? What happened? Is this a story that you can laugh about now, even though it was incredibly embarrassing or frustrating at the time?

Commentary

"All we like sheep have gone astray; we have turned every one to his own way" (Isaiah 53:6a). So many times in our lives, we are just as dumb as sheep. We so boldly choose sin to control our lives that we wonder how it could ever be true that we will ever experience life eternal with Jesus. That's when we need to be reminded, "For by grace you have been saved through faith. And this is not your own doing; it is the gift of God" (Ephesians 2:8). So when the day comes for Jesus to separate the sheep from the goats, those who have received faith will be saved, like sheep.

To the goats, those unbelievers, we sheep seem dumb for an entirely different reason. 1 Corinthians 1:18 says, "For the message of the cross is foolishness to those who are perishing, but to us who are being saved it is the power of God" (NIV). A "goat" is a "goat" in the first place because it refuses to believe that it is only through Jesus Christ's death and resurrection that we are saved. A "goat" would rather trust its own ability to save. A "goat" doesn't need a Savior. To a "goat," a nail-pierced Savior doesn't make sense.

For this reason, I just wanna be a sheep! Faith in Jesus is really quite simple: the Bible says it! Through the gift of faith, I believe it! And on that final day, I will enjoy Jesus' profile from the right side!

Concordance

Find additional verses that apply to this devotion. Possible key words include *Sheep, Shepherd, Goat,* and *Separate.* Or read:

> *Again, the kingdom of heaven is like a net that was thrown into the sea and gathered fish of every kind. When it was full, men drew it ashore and sat down and sorted the good into containers but threw away the bad. So it will be at the close of the age. The angels will come out and separate the evil from the righteous and throw*

> *them into the fiery furnace. In that place there will be weeping and gnashing of teeth (Matthew 13:47–50).*

_____

_____

_____

_____

_____

Meditate

Ask participants to listen carefully as you read one or more additional verses. Allow time for them to meditate on the meaning of these words of Scripture. After a couple of moments, close with prayer.

Prayer Springboard

Holy Shepherd, thank You for calling us to be sheep in Your flock. You have called all people to Yourself. Use us to tell others about You so that they may live with You for all eternity in heaven. . . .

_____

_____

_____

_____

_____

Date used _____

Used for _____

49

Running or Resting?

Scripture Springboard

He who dwells in the shelter of the Most High will rest in the shadow of the Almighty. I will say of the Lord, "He is my refuge and my fortress, my God, in whom I trust." . . . He will cover you with His feathers, and under His wings you will find refuge; His faithfulness will be your shield and rampart (Psalm 91:1–2, 4 NIV).

Activity

The ideal setting for this activity is outside in a field with some scattered trees. Play a simple game of tag in which one person is "it" and the trees serve as bases. As long as you're touching a tree, you can't be tagged. Once tagged, that person becomes "it." Afterward, ask the following questions: What was it like to be touching base? What was it like to be away from base? In your spiritual life, according to Psalm 91, what is base?

_____

_____

_____

_____

_____

Commentary

Your heart pounds and your lungs heave as you run from whatever chases you. You've run for days, months, sometimes even years. You just want the running and chasing to be over. You are tired. You need rest. Where will you go? To whom can you turn?

Personal Story

When have you felt chased, either physically or spiritually? Are you still running? What or who is chasing you? Is there an end in sight? Where or to whom will you go for relief and protection?

_____

_____

_____

_____

_____

Commentary

Every person in this room knows the feeling of running from something. Sometimes people run from responsibility, maturity, reality, or truth. There is no honor in that, for the running will continue and real joy will never come. But what about those who are consistently running from Satan and sin's grasp? Do you remember the dark times in your life? No matter how fast you ran, sin always seemed to be grabbing at your ankle. Even sharp turns and quick moves couldn't free you because Satan seemed to know your thoughts and was always one step ahead of you.

Then you heard the sweet voice of Jesus: "I'm coming!" And just at that moment when Satan's gnarled fingers tightened around your ankle with a fierce grip, Jesus appeared and gathered you up into His protective arms and said, "No, Satan! This one is Mine!" Then Jesus looked at you with His compassionate eyes and tenderly whispered, "You're safe." That is what it means to dwell with the Most High (v. 1), to call the Lord your refuge and fortress (v. 2), to be covered by His feathers, and to take refuge under His mighty wing (v. 4).

Now, Jesus bids us stay. So often we climb down from His arms and start running again, teasing Satan to chase us. Once again, Jesus invites us to stay in His arms, where true safety and protection are ours!

Concordance

Find one more verse that applies to this devotion. Possible key words include *Shelter*, *Protection*, and *Fortress*. Or read:

> He said, "The LORD is my rock and
> my fortress and my deliverer, my
> God, my rock, in whom I take
> refuge, my shield, and the horn of
> my salvation, my stronghold and
> my refuge, my savior; You save me

*from violence. I call upon the
LORD, who is worthy to be praised,
and I am saved from my enemies"
(2 Samuel 22:2–4).*

_____
_____
_____
_____
_____

Meditate

Listen closely to this final verse and meditate on its meaning. After a couple of moments, close with prayer.

Prayer Springboard

Dear God, we praise You for being our mighty stronghold, an ever-present help in time of trouble. . . .

_____
_____
_____
_____
_____

50

First to Know

Scripture Springboard

And in the same region there were shepherds out in the field, keeping watch over their flock by night. And an angel of the Lord appeared to them, and the glory of the Lord shone around them, and they were filled with fear. And the angel said to them, "Fear not, for behold, I bring you good news of a great joy that will be for all the people" (Luke 2:8–10).

Activity

Today's task is simply to choose teams. You don't even need to have another activity; just choose two captains and ask them to take turns picking members for their teams. Once the last person has been picked, ask these questions: What was it like to be picked early? What was it like to be picked last?

_____

_____

_____

_____

Commentary

If the wind was blowing just right, you could smell the shepherds' stench from a mile away. Truth be told, the sheep were cleaner than the shepherds. For weeks at a time, the shepherds tended their flocks. Baths in the river or lake simply weren't a priority. "Who should I impress? The sheep don't care that I smell or am unclean," thought the lowly shepherd.

Personal Story

Tell the group about a time when you felt unimportant. Can you think of a time when you were picked last? What was that like for you?

_____

_____

_____

_____

Commentary

Suppose that you had been one of the shepherds on the eve of Jesus' birth. Close your eyes and imagine it for a moment: It was night, and the only sound for miles around was the heavy breathing of the sleeping sheep. An occasional grumble or snort is heard from the shepherd sleeping a few yards from you; he must be dreaming again. You can't sleep, so you wonder why you are here, in a place you never dreamed or hoped to be. As a kid, you admired the woodworkers in the villages so much. You knew that you would grow up and be apprenticed to the woodworking shop. But when the time came, you weren't wanted. You tried to learn other trades, but too many mistakes have led you here: sleeping in a dirty field, with dirtier sheep, next to the dirtiest shepherd. You sigh deeply and whisper, "How did I end up here?"

Suddenly, a light brighter than the sun blinds your tired, weary eyes. "What is that?! Is that an angel?! What did he say? But why are you telling *us* all this? Don't you know we're only dumb shepherds? Go where?! To the town of David and find what? A Savior! You mean we're the first to know? The angel told *us* first?!"

For the first time, you feel special—but more important, and oddly enough, you feel saved. "Let us go over to Bethlehem and see this thing that has happened, which the Lord has made known to us!" You start to run, then stop as you consider your own words. "He told *us*, shepherds . . . amazing!"

Concordance

Find one more verse that applies to this devotion. Possible key words include *Angel*, *Nativity*, and *Manger*. Or read:

> *When the angels went away from them into heaven, the shepherds said to one another, "Let us go over to Bethlehem and see this thing that has happened, which the Lord has made known to us." And they went with haste and found Mary and Joseph, and the baby lying in a manger. And*

> *when they saw it, they made known the saying that had been told them concerning this child. And all who heard it wondered at what the shepherds told them. But Mary treasured up all these things, pondering them in her heart. And the shepherds returned, glorifying and praising God for all they had heard and seen, as it had been told them (Luke 2:15–20).*

_____

_____

_____

_____

Meditate

Listen closely to this final verse and meditate on its meaning. After a couple of moments, close with prayer.

Prayer Springboard

Dear Lord, thank You for picking the shepherds and for choosing us. Most important, thank You for sending Your perfect Son, Jesus, into the world to redeem us from our sins. . . .

_____

_____

_____

_____

51

Righteousness over Revenge

Scripture Springboard

Now the birth of Jesus Christ took place in this way. When His mother Mary had been betrothed to Joseph, before they came together she was found to be with child from the Holy Spirit. And her husband Joseph, being a just man and unwilling to put her to shame, resolved to divorce her quietly (Matthew 1:18–19).

Activity

Get a deck of Uno cards. Take out all of the numbered cards and set them in the center to draw from. Deal out the rest of the "revenge" cards so that everyone has the same number. Choose someone to start, and let the game begin. Create an atmosphere of intense revenge: "You want me to Draw Two? Fine! You can Draw Four!" Play until someone runs out of cards and is declared the winner.

_____

_____

_____

_____

Commentary

Revenge is an ugly outfit, but we all wear it so well. Doesn't today's Scripture reading amaze you? Joseph chose righteousness rather than revenge. Praise God that He chose Joseph to be the earthly father of Jesus Christ!

Personal Story

Tell the group about the most righteous man that you can think of. Why do you feel this way? What have you learned from him, and how do you apply it to your daily life?

_____

_____

_____

_____

_____

Commentary

Put yourself in Joseph's shoes for a moment, and consider what you would have done. You're pledged to be married to your young and beautiful bride, only to find out that she is pregnant! You might think, "Why would she do this to me? Who is the father? What can I do to get revenge?" You and I might have exposed Mary and her "sin," leading to certain public disgrace. "That will teach her to mess with me," we would probably think. But what does Joseph do? Because he is a righteous man, he chooses to divorce her quietly.

Then, while Joseph's head swirls with confusion and hurt, an angel of the Lord comes to him in a dream during his time of need. Isn't the Lord just like that? When we need God the most, He comes to us quickly with words of help, comfort, and encouragement in His Holy Word and in the promise made in the Sacraments. Another sign of Joseph's faithfulness is found in Matthew 1:24: "When Joseph woke up, he did what the angel of the Lord had commanded him and took Mary home as his wife" (NIV). In faith, Joseph did what the angel told him to do. He was obedient to the will of God. Joseph was the right man to be the earthly father of our Savior, Jesus. That must be why God chose him.

Concordance

Find one or more verses that apply to this devotion. Possible key words include *Righteous, Obedient,* and *Joseph.* Or read:

Have this mind among yourselves, which is yours in Christ Jesus, who, though He was in the form of God, did not count equality with God a thing to be grasped, but made Himself nothing, taking the form of a servant, being born in the likeness of men. And being found in human form, He humbled Himself by becoming obedient to the point of death, even death on a cross. Therefore God has highly exalted Him and bestowed on Him the name that is above every name, so that at the name of Jesus every knee should bow, in heaven and on earth and under the earth, and every tongue confess that Jesus Christ is Lord, to the glory of God the Father (Philippians 2:5–11).

_____
_____
_____
_____
_____

Meditate

Have participants listen closely to this final verse and meditate on its meaning. After a couple of moments, close with prayer.

Prayer Springboard

Dear God, we praise You for the gift of Your Son, Jesus. We praise You that You provided faith to Joseph in his time of confusion and trouble. Help us to read and understand Your promises to us in Your Word. . . .

_____
_____
_____
_____

52

God's Perfect Plan

Scripture Springboard

For all have sinned and fall short of the glory of God, and are justified by His grace as a gift, through the redemption that is in Christ Jesus (Romans 3:23–24).

Therefore, just as sin came into the world through one man, and death through sin, and so death spread to all men because all sinned (Romans 5:12).

Activity

This activity belongs to Christ and not to you or me.

You see, at just the right time, when we were still powerless, Christ died for the ungodly. . . . God demonstrates His own love for us in this: While we were still sinners, Christ died for us (Romans 5:6, 8 NIV).

It was now about the sixth hour, and darkness came over the whole land until the ninth hour, for the sun stopped shining. And the curtain of the temple was torn in two. Jesus called out with a loud voice, "Father into your hands I commit My spirit." When He had said this, He breathed His last (Luke 23:44–46 NIV).

Commentary

For God so loved the world, that He gave His only Son, that whoever believes in Him should not perish but have eternal life. For God did not send His Son into the world to condemn the world, but in order that the world might be saved through Him (John 3:16–17).

Personal Story

Share with the group the moment when you first believed in Jesus Christ. Maybe you've always been a Christian. Share with them a time when you confirmed your belief in Jesus Christ. What was that experience like? How has your life been different?

_____
_____
_____
_____
_____
_____

Commentary

Now I would remind you, brothers, of the gospel I preached to you, which you received, in which you stand, and by which you are being saved, if you hold fast to the word I preached to you—unless you believed in vain. For I delivered to you as of first importance what I also received: that Christ died for our sins in accordance with the Scriptures, that He was buried, that He was raised on the third day in accordance with the Scriptures, and that He appeared to Cephas, then to the twelve (1 Corinthians 15:1–5).

Concordance

Find one more verse that applies to this devotion. Possible key words include *Salvation, Cross,* and *Resurrection.* Or read:

Jesus said to her, "I am the resurrection and the life. Whoever believes in Me, though he die, yet shall he live, and everyone who lives and believes in Me shall never die." (John 11:25–26a).

Meditate

Listen closely to this final verse and meditate on its meaning in your life. After a couple of moments, pray together.

Prayer Springboard

Dear Jesus, we believe in You. Thank You for delivering us from our sins. Please send Your Spirit to enter in and daily lead us by Your true Word. . . .

_____
_____
_____
_____
_____